I0141844

"Let the Earth Bring Forth": Evolution and Scripture

Howard C. Stutz

Greg Kofford Books
Salt Lake City, Utah
2011

©2010 by Howard C. Stutz

Cover design copyrighted © 2010 by Greg Kofford Books, Inc.

Published in the USA

All rights reserved. No part of this volume may be reproduced in any form without written permission from the publisher, Greg Kofford Books. The views expressed herein are the responsibility of the author and do not necessarily represent the position of Greg Kofford Books, Inc.

2014 13 12 11   5 4 3 2 1

Greg Kofford Books, Inc.
P.O. Box 1362
Draper, UT 84020
www.koffordbooks.com

Library of Congress Cataloging-in-Publication Data

Stutz, Howard C.
    Let the earth bring forth : evolution and Scripture / Howard C. Stutz.
        p. cm.
    Includes index.
    ISBN 978-1-58958-126-5
    1. Evolution--Religious aspects--Church of Jesus Christ of Latter-day Saints. I. Title.
    BX8643.R39S78 2010
    231.7'652--dc22
                                    2010018709

To my wife, Mildred

CONTENTS

Foreword by Duane E. Jeffery   vii

Acknowledgments   xv

Introduction   xvii

Chapter

1	"Opposition in All Things"	1
2	New Species from Mutations	9
3	New Species from Sexual Recombination	15
4	Speciation in Plants by Polyploidy	19
5	The Fossil Record	25
6	Distribution Patterns as Evidence for Evolution	31
7	Embryological Evidence for Evolution	41
8	Comparative Anatomy as Evidence for Evolution	47
9	Biochemical Evidence	55
10	Genetic Evidence	59
11	The Quest for Truth	63
12	"And the Lord God Formed Man"	71
13	Evolution and the Scriptures	77
Subject Index		81
Scripture Index		87
About the Author		89

Foreword

Duane E. Jeffery

"Speak to the earth, and it shall teach thee."
—Job 12:8

Job's counsel is good: The earth and its organisms may indeed teach us things of divine import. The concept was expanded in 1605 by Francis Bacon, the English philosopher and statesman who is considered one of the first to really "think about thinking" and who laid the foundations of our modern methods of logic and mental analysis. Bacon asserted that we can learn of divine things from either of two "books": "Let no man…think or maintain, that a man can search too far, or be too well studied in the book of God's word, or in the book of God's works, divinity or philosophy, but rather let men endeavour an endless progress or proficience in both."[1] Philosophy, in his day, encompassed all of what we today call science—the study of the physical and natural world.

And Charles Darwin chose that passage from Bacon to set the stage for the title page of his major work *On the Origin of Species*.

The "Two Books Doctrine," as it has become known, has been used many times since 1605 by religious scientists seeking to convey their insights to a public which is often reluctant to study and accept the realities of the natural world. And it is fitting that *Let the Earth Bring Forth* was written in 2009, the 200th anniversary of Darwin's birth and the 150th of the publication of *The Origin*. (It is also the 400th anniversary of Galileo's first

studies with the telescope.) So it seems appropriate here to summarize where Christianity in particular has come with the relationships between science and religion in the intervening years.

In brief, the story is a stressful one, generally depicted as a
long slow retreat by religious doctrines in the face of an ever-
expanding and demonstrable science. Catholicism made the
mistake of formally condemning Galileo for heresy and has
been trying repeatedly ever since to establish that the Church is
not anti-science. Indeed the Catholic Church has maintained its
own observatory, the Vatican Observatory, for over two centuries now. Protestant leaders varied on the new ideas. Luther
publicly called Copernicus a fool. But eventually it became clear
that the heliocentric, sun-centered, view of our solar system
was indeed correct. Though everyone saw the sun "rise" every
morning, it became clear that it was really a rotating earth that
brought the sun into view; the sun itself had nothing whatever
to do with sunrise and sunset. Numerous biblical passages had
to be read with new understanding to accommodate the idea
that what our eyes so plainly told us was really an illusion.

And this process validated a further comment from Bacon
regarding the Two Books. Said he: "Our Saviour saith, 'You err,
not knowing the Scriptures, nor the power of God, laying
before us two books or volumes to study, if we will be secured
from error; first the Scriptures, revealing the will of God, and
then the creatures expressing his power; whereof the latter is a
key unto the former . . . opening our understanding to con-
ceive the true sense of the Scriptures."[2] The latter is a key to
the former. That idea took hold widely in Christendom, as far
as the solar system was concerned.

But then came Darwin's *The Origin* in 1859, and the
stresses arose again quickly and with even greater intensity.
Darwin tried to explain in his book that he saw no good reason
why the book's ideas should disturb religious feelings and
quoted a noted clergyman of the day to the effect that it was a
nobler view of deity to think of God having created laws which
themselves brought about creation than to think that He
Himself had to make everything directly. Still, evolution by nat-

ural selection was not an easy concept for many people to accept. Numerous historians have pointed out that Darwin was challenged more vigorously by scientists than he was by religionists; and to a certain extent, that is true

Darwin was denounced in 1860 by the Anglican bishop Samuel Wilberforce (and defended by Thomas Henry Huxley), but this episode has been given far more publicity than it merits in attempts to show that religion and science were quickly and rather inextricably locked in combat. The truth is that Darwin had numerous supporters in religious circles. At his death the family intended to bury him on the family estate, but the Anglican Church proffered space in its most hallowed cemetery, Westminster Abbey. And there Darwin is interred, only a few paces from the much-revered Isaac Newton. A canon of the Church was among Darwin's pallbearers, and memorial sermons were preached in various churches extolling his contributions.

This is not to say that Darwin in his maturity was a believer in the religious doctrines of his day. He came to characterize himself as agnostic, feeling that the huge questions of religion were too far beyond the mind of man to be satisfactorily resolved. Yet he saw no reason why his ideas should be seen as inimical to overall religious faith.

But various attempts to forge a synthesis of his views with the basics of biblical Christianity proved not of widespread appeal. In the early twentieth century, a few religionists in America decided it was necessary to identify what really were, in their view, the absolute basics of Christianity, the solid fundamentals. This effort led to a series of publications in the century's second decade understandably termed "The Fundamentals." About a fifth of these discussions deal quite directly with evolution. These publications gave rise to the "Christian fundamentalists" still with us today, who espouse such ideas as that the earth is less than ten thousand years old, that species do not change, and that evolution is false or even a Satanic counterfeit for the gospel.

Most of the major Christian denominations, both Protestant and Catholic, have since Darwin's day come to considerable peace with the concept that God is indeed capable of establishing natural laws that can generate new species and the entire world of biological diversity. Formal statements by numerous such organizations may be found in Carrie Sager, ed., *Voices for Evolution*, 3d ed. (Berkeley, Calif: National Center for Science Education, 2008). Others remain opposed, however, and these views keep our present society busy debating a proper place for these dissenting ideas in the public school system. Both modern Young Earth Creationists (YEC) and proponents of that group's offshoot, Intelligent Design, try to use scientific arguments to give validity and respectability to their religiously generated views, but those arguments have not found fertile ground in either the scientific establishment at large or in the courts.

But what about Mormonism? The statements made by, or authorized for publication by, the First Presidency of the Church may be readily accessed in William E. Evenson and Duane E. Jeffery, eds., *Mormonism and Evolution: The Authoritative LDS Statements* (Salt Lake City: Greg Kofford Books, 2006). The basic story is that the First Presidency, the sole source of authoritative statements, first addressed the subject one hundred years ago in 1909, on the centennial of Darwin's birth and almost precisely on the fiftieth anniversary of the publication of *The Origin of Species*. The 1909 statement contains a brief passage which is quite clearly anti-evolutionary in tone.

But five months later (April 1910) came an expanded response to questions regarding the origin of the bodies of Adam and Eve, that suggested three apparently acceptable possibilities for this origin. First was divinely directed evolution by natural processes, second was transplantation from other spheres, and third was "born here in mortality as other mortals have been."[3] These three possibilities were left open, without resolution. Subsequent authoritative statements moved progressively to an even more open position; the latest communications known to me from the First Presidency's office assert only that humans are created in the image of God. The mechanisms of that creation are left unaddressed.[4]

A major doctrinal dispute developed in the late 1920s and early 1930s, culminating in a formal meeting of all General Authorities on April 7, 1931. In that meeting, the First Presidency declared that the Church took no position on the two major points under discussion: whether there had, or had not, been death on earth before the fall of Adam, and whether there had, or had not, been human-like beings on earth prior to the time of Adam (so-called pre-Adamites). The Church formally disavowed alignment with either side of these two issues and pointedly enjoined all General Authorities to leave the subject alone.[5]

Most have done so, but a few have moved beyond the First Presidency's counsel to attack evolution. This development, remarkably, has rather swung considerable numbers of LDS people to consider themselves aligned more with the views of the Young Earth Creationists. Any quick examination of those views will reveal virtually total disagreement between LDS theology and the YEC groups; indeed it is from those quarters that the most common and dogmatic attacks on the Church originate.[6]

Without question, Mormon writers have produced many anti-evolution, indeed anti-science, books, often borrowing arguments from the YEC camp in an appeal for scientific respectability. But other works have taken a much more favorable view, including several by well-established and respected LDS scientists. Among such authors are geologists Frederick J. Pack, James E. Talmage, and William Lee Stokes, botanist Frank B. Salisbury, and embryologist Trent D. Stephens co-authoring with vertebrate anatomist D. Jeffrey Meldrum. Pack and Talmage, at least, openly invoked Bacon's Two Books Doctrine, but that insight seems to have not to have caught on well in LDS commentary.

And now comes the first book by an LDS evolutionary biologist in the strict sense of the term. Howard C. Stutz, emeritus professor of genetics at Brigham Young University, indeed finds Earth's organisms to be a "key" to understanding the more usual book of God, the scriptures. Brother Stutz has spent a long and productive career studying the evolution of the plants of western North America but, in addition, has spent extensive time studying the native plants of the Middle East including those on the slopes of Mount Ararat. He has had an incredibly varied career: Golden Gloves boxing champion and coach, high school teacher and principal, soldier with Patton's Third Army in World War II, and biology professor at both the college and university levels. He received his doctoral training under the world's leading evolutionary plant biologist of that day, G. Ledyard Stebbins at the University of California, Berkeley. With his graduate-level courses, he brought the first formal training in evolution to students at BYU. His professional stature was instrumental in the decision of the U.S. Forest Service to establish a formal research laboratory adjacent to the BYU campus, dedicated to studying the evolution and ecology of desert shrubs of the West.

In the Church he has filled numerous positions, including service as a high councilor (three times), bishop, and stake patriarch. Truly this is a man intimately familiar on a very personal level with both books of Deity. We are privileged to have in this book, his views gained over a lifetime of study, as he shares his conclusions about how the earth has indeed "brought forth."

Notes

1. Francis Bacon, *Advancement of Learning, Book I*, in *Great Books of the Western World*, editor in chief Robert Maynard Hutchins (Chicago: University of Chicago Press, 1952), 30:4.

2. Ibid., 30:20.

3. "Origin of Man," directive in First Presidency's message, *Improvement Era* 13 (April 1910): 570; see also William E. Evenson and Duane E. Jeffery, *Mormonism and Evolution: The Authoritative LDS Statements* (Salt Lake City: Greg Kofford Books, 2006), 43–44.

4. Evenson and Jeffery, *Mormonism and Evolution*, 42–114.

5. First Presidency, Memo to other General Authorities, April 5, 1931, in ibid., 54–67; see also Willam E. Evenson, "Evolution," *Encyclopedia of Mormonism* (New York: Macmillan Company, 1992),

2:478. This encyclopedia article is included in the Church-approved BYU packet, "Origin of Man and Evolution."

6. Young Earth Creationism draws its proponents from a variety of Protestant faiths, among which Southern Baptists are probably the most prominent. YECs have steadfastly declined to produce a point-by-point outline of their communal faith, but the basics can be identified in many different sources. Prominent doctrines include belief in *ex nihilo* and fiat creation (that, from nothing, God spoke all time, space, and matter into existence some six to ten thousand years ago), that the creation days of Genesis were six literal twenty-four-hour days, that Adam was created literally from an accumulation of dust and Eve was made from his excised rib. All these fundamentals have been pointedly rejected by LDS prophets, and such a literal reading of Genesis was notably not included among the three apparently acceptable "possibilities" for human origins spelled out in the First Presidency's April 1910 directive (see note 3). A very concise summary of YEC teachings, though it was not intended as such, is in Richard Niessen, "Several Significant Discrepancies between Theistic Evolution and the Biblical Account," *Creation Research Society Quarterly* 16 (March 1980): 222ff.

Acknowledgments

This essay was prepared to help point out the harmony which exists between the theory of speciation by organic evolution and revealed truths contained in the holy scriptures. It results from numerous discussions with students of nearly all ages, but primarily with those of college age. Because nearly everyone who has responded to these discussions has expressed gratitude for how helpfully these concepts harmonized scientific discoveries with gospel truths, I have been motivated to publish them in hopes that they may serve a wider audience. I sincerely hope that those who read it will have their testimony of the truthfulness of the gospel and of the reality of God thereby strengthened.

I wish it were possible to express gratitude to each of the many individuals who have assisted in the preparation of this essay; but since their contributions are so reticulately interwoven with ideas and contributions of so many associates and teachers, it would be impossible to identify each of them. There are, however, a few individuals who have contributed so much to my understanding and to the motivation required for me to carry these concepts through to publication that I would like to acknowledge with thanks their valuable assistance and influence.

I owe a great deal to the late G. L. Stebbins, professor of genetics and evolutionary biology at the University of California, who not only taught me much of what I know about evolutionary thought but who repeatedly required me to test these concepts against my religious faith. I am also indebted to many former colleagues including Duane E. Jeffery, professor emeritus of zoology and integrative biology at Brigham Young University, Daniel J. Fairbanks, professor of genetics and associate dean at Utah Valley University, and Berthold O. Bergh, professor emeritus of genetics at the University of California, Riverside. I am grateful to my daughter Ellen Landeen who has spent many hours editing and improving the language of many of the concepts, as well as to the scores of students from whom I invited challenges to these concepts and from whom I have received many helpful insights.

More than to all others, I am indebted to my gracious wife, Mildred. Not only has she supported me and patiently listened to me repeat many of these concepts at numerous informal fireside chat presentations and public lectures, but she has tactfully guided me away from many dead-end concepts and into new exciting discoveries. I would that every author could be similarly blessed with such a wise sounding-board and companion.

Introduction

"In the beginning, God created the heavens and the earth."
—Genesis 1:1

This powerful and majestic declaration not only introduces the message of the Bible but also fairly well summarizes it. It is the message of all of the great prophets: God is the author and omnipotent creator of all things. The Book of Mormon repeats this message of God as creator: "Behold, I am Jesus Christ the Son of God. I created the heavens and the earth, and all things that in them are. I was with the Father from the beginning . . . I am the light and the life of the world. I am Alpha and Omega, the beginning and the end" (3 Ne. 9:15, 18). God is the creator of everything including all the non-living components of the heavens as well as the multitude of living organisms brought forth from the Earth.

This creation may have been accomplished by two distinctly different episodes: (1) the creation of the heavens, and (2) the creation of the Earth. According to scientists, the creation of the heavens began in a split second approximately 13–14 billion years ago with what has commonly been called the "Big Bang," resulting in the formation of galaxies, planets, suns, stars and all other non-living creations in the universe. Geological records indicate that the Earth was formed about four billion years ago. However, the creation of our tiny planet was unique. It provided the conditions necessary for all living organisms to come forth as planned by God in the beginning. Endowed with specific attributes, it enabled the fulfillment of

God's plan, whereby His spirit children could come, obtain bodies, work out their salvation and attain eternal life. God created the Earth to fulfill His purposes: "For behold, this is my work and my glory—to bring to pass the immortality and eternal life of man" (Moses 1:39).

In speaking with Abraham, God indicated that living organisms would emerge from the Earth:

> And the Gods said: Let us prepare the earth to bring forth grass; the herb yielding seed; the fruit tree yielding fruit after his kind, whose seed in itself yieldeth its own likeness upon the earth; and it was so, even as they ordered.
>
> And the Gods organized the earth to bring forth grass from its own seed, and the herb to bring forth herb from its own seed, yielding seed after his kind; and the earth to bring forth the tree from its own seed, yielding fruit whose seed could only bring forth the same in itself, after his kind; and the Gods saw that they were obeyed. (Abr. 4:11–12)

Life first appeared on Earth about 3 billion years ago. For the next 2 billion years, life was confined primarily to anaerobic blue-green algae and bacteria. Subsequently, other forms of life became dominant including fish and insects, flowering plants and forests, reptiles and mammals, and eventually human beings.

The process by which the Earth gave rise to living organisms is what is generally referred to now as the process of organic evolution.

"Do you believe in evolution?" The ambiguity of this oft-asked question is made conspicuous by parallel questions such as "Do you believe in photosynthesis? Or osmosis? Or respiration?" Asking such questions poses them as creeds instead of processes. As with other phenomena, evolution is a process, not a creed. Just as photosynthesis is the process whereby light energy is changed to chemical energy, organic evolution is the process whereby biological species are formed.

Most scientists accept the process of evolution as the avenue by which all biological species are created. These scientists are often referred to as "evolutionists." Others who accept only the literal biblical account are identified as "creationists" and hold that, by divine intervention, God created each species *de novo*. Between these two positions are many variations, encompassing various degrees of divine intervention in the creation process.

One of the greatest tragedies in recent times has been the extensive promulgation of creeds that have created chasms between science and religion. At no time in the history of humankind has science provided a more comprehensible panorama of the universe in which we live. Nor has there ever been a time when God has more clearly revealed Himself and His purposes to His children. Why then should there be so much apparent conflict between science and religion?

Some have found scientific discoveries to be so enchanting and all-powerful that they have supposed that God is actually a human creation, rather than vice versa. Just as naive and unproductive have been the expressions of some who find scientific theories to be "of the devil" and to be avoided with a passion. As a consequence of such prejudice, far too many people have denied themselves both the blessings available from revelations emanating from our laboratories as well as revelations given to us through our prophets. But all truth must eventually be completely harmonious and compatible, for the scriptures tell us that the "glory of God is intelligence, or, in other words, light and truth" (D&C 93:36). There can be no permanent impasse between human discoveries and those provided by the Lord through revelation; they are all His. Apparent conflicts are due either to ignorance or to misinterpretation.

Our scientific discoveries accumulate so rapidly that theories are altered and refined from one decade to the next. Our concept of light, of electricity, of ionizing radiation, of molecules and atoms and stars and galaxies and universes are conspicuously different from what they were a short time ago. A few hundred years ago, because of statements in the Bible by Joshua, it was accepted as fact that the sun revolved around the Earth:

Sun, stand thou still upon Gibeon; and thou, moon, in
the valley of Ajalon.

And the sun stood still, and the moon stayed, until the
people had avenged themselves upon their enemies. Is not
this written in the book of Jasher? So the sun stood still in
the midst of heaven, and hasted not to go down about a
whole day. (Josh. 10:12–13)

This statement was taken as irrefutable testimony that the
Earth was the center of the universe and that the sun revolved
around the Earth. Those who dared to challenge this interpretation were severely ridiculed and often even physically punished.

When Polish astronomer Nicholas Copernicus suggested
in 1543 that the sun was the center of the solar system and that
it was the rotation of the Earth in reference to the stationary
sun which gave us alternate periods of day and night, many theologians were outraged. As Father Inchofer, a Jesuit priest and
professor of mathematics and theology in Sicily, expressed it in
1616, "The opinion of the earth's motion is of all heresies the
most abominable, the most scandalous; the immobility of the
earth is thrice sacred; argument against the immortality of the
soul, the existence of God, and the incarnation should be toler-
ated sooner than an argument to prove the earth moves."[1]

Martin Luther, the powerful German theologian, professor, and pastor, who launched the Reformation during the early
1500s, expressed his rancor this way: "People give ear to an
upstart astrologer, [Copernicus], who strove to show that the
earth revolves, not the heavens or the firmament, the sun and
the moon. Whoever wishes to appear clever must devise some
new system, which of all systems is, of course, the very best.
This fool wishes to reverse the entire science of astronomy, but
sacred scripture tells us that Joshua commanded the sun to
stand still, and not the earth."[2]

Many sincere God-fearing persons had attached their testimonies so firmly to one interpretation of the scriptures that
they were unable to adjust to the irrefutable evidences that
accumulated to prove the movement of the Earth.

Consequently some abandoned all other revelations from God and put their trust solely in human philosophies.

The controversy over organic evolution has been as severe as the controversy over Copernican astronomy, but the scriptures themselves seldom furnish any direct basis for such conflicts. It is usually only because of traditional interpretations that argument continues.

Until recent times, almost everyone regarded all of the species of plants and animals on Earth as immutable, true-breeding forms that had always existed unchanged since their creation. According to the Creationists, God created each species individually and instantaneously. This interpretation may stem from the wording in the first line of Genesis in the King James Version of the Bible, which states, "In the beginning God created the heaven and the earth." It is interesting to note that the Hebrew Bible translates this phrase as "be-re-SHIYT ba-RA eh-lo-HIYM," which literally reads, "in beginning God created (the heavens and the earth).[3] Remarkably, the omission of the word "the" changes the emphasis of the creation process from a single event as accepted by creationists to a process as proposed by evolutionists. Evolutionists understand creation to be a continuing process of speciation from ancestral forms, stretching over eons of time, which has produced all species of plants and animals on Earth today as well as those which are now extinct and those which will undoubtedly come forth in the future. As expressed by the English scientist and naturalist Charles Darwin in 1859, all living organisms on Earth are influenced by natural selection in the process of creating new species. The essential biblical expression of this process is "Let the earth bring forth" (Gen. 1:24).

> And God created great whales, and every living creature that moveth, which the *waters brought forth* abundantly, after their kind, and winged fowl after his kind: and God saw that it was good. (Gen. 1:21)
> And *out of the ground* the Lord God formed every beast of the field and every fowl of the air; and brought them unto Adam to see what he would call them: and whatsoever

Adam called every living creature, that was the name thereof. (Gen. 2:19)

And God said, Let the *earth bring forth* the living creature after his kind. (Gen. 1:24)

Let the *waters bring forth* abundantly. (Gen. 1:20)

God prepared the Earth to bring forth. "Let the earth bring forth" and "let the waters bring forth." It could not have been stated much more plainly nor much more emphatically. These phrases were repeated five times in the first chapter of Genesis.

Today we are aware of many new species coming into existence from the Earth and from the waters. In recent recorded history, we have also seen the demise of several species and are witnessing the extinction of many others. The creation process set in motion with the creation of the Earth is a never-ending, eternal process. This process, known today as organic evolution, is what the scriptures describe, and it is also what we have learned in our scientific studies.

Notes

1. Father Inchofer, quoted in Andrew Dickson White, *A History of the Warfare of Science with Theology in Christendom* (New York: D. Appleton and Company, 1898), 398.

2. Martin Luther, quoted in Laura Fermi and Gilberto Bernardini, *Galileo and the Scientific Revolution* (Mineola, N.Y.: Dover Publications, 2003), 75.

3. Bonnie Pedrotti Kittel, Vicki Hoffer, and Rebecca Abts Wright, *Biblical Hebrew: A Text and Workbook* (Ithaca, N.Y.: Yale University Press, 1989).

1
"Opposition in All Things"

No two spots on Earth are identical. They cannot be. Each is larger or smaller, warmer or cooler, wetter or drier than others. The extensive array of conditions that shapes the physical world is reflected in the numerous living organisms that occupy each environment. Those which live in deserts differ from those living on stream banks. Those living on mountain slopes differ from those that occupy valleys. Even individuals living side by side differ. Cells, organs, tissues, and organelles within each individual differ. Not only are there no identical spots on Earth but every spot is constantly changing. Moment by moment, hour by hour, day by day, everything changes.

The Book of Mormon prophet Lehi explained to his son the need for opposition for life even to exist. There could be no flesh—no life or death—without opposition:

> For it must needs be, that there is an opposition in all things. If not so, my first-born in the wilderness, righteousness could not be brought to pass, neither wickedness, neither holiness nor misery, neither good nor bad. Wherefore, all things must needs be a compound in one; wherefore, if it should be one body it must needs remain as dead, having no life neither death, nor corruption nor incorruption, happiness nor misery, neither sense nor insensibility.
>
> Wherefore, it must needs have been created for a thing of naught; wherefore there would have been no purpose in the end of its creation. (2 Ne. 2:11–12)

Adam could not have existed without the opportunity for a choice of life or death. He could not have been obedient if disobedience were not a possibility.

Throughout the universe reigns the all-encompassing principle of opposition in all things. Every thing that *is* is identified by contiguous *is not*. A finger is a finger because of contiguous non-finger tissue. A pebble is a pebble because it is surrounded by contiguous non-pebble; a galaxy is a galaxy because it is bounded by contiguous non-galaxy, and non-universe space defines a universe. Everything is defined by its contiguous absence. Likewise, the universal principle of opposition in all things is expressed in the process of natural selection. Much as a sculptor creates a marble statue by removal, so does natural selection create species of living organisms by removal.

The severe challenge for living organisms to survive the infinitely variable, constantly changing, environments of planet Earth is accommodated in two ways: (1) phenotypic plasticity and (2) genetic flexibility.

Phenotypic Plasticity

Plasticity is the capacity of an individual organism to change attributes as the environment changes. Because everything is constantly changing, no organism can exist without sufficient plasticity to accommodate the changes. When plasticity is insufficient to accommodate the accompanying environmental changes which will inevitably come, death ensues.

For example, when the environment requisite to the survival of dinosaurs changed, dinosaurs became extinct. Likewise, trilobites all died out because of their inability to accommodate a new environment. Thousands of species were extinguished when the landscapes of the Earth were destroyed by extensive glaciers during the ice age. The fossil record is replete with examples of thousands, even millions, of now-extinct species of plants and animals which had insufficient plasticity to meet their new challenges.

Since long lifespans require more plasticity for survival, long-lived organisms are generally more plastic than those with short life-spans. Perennial plants usually require more plasticity than annuals, permitting them to survive challenges over a longer time period. Because microorganisms are short lived, they generally have little plasticity, succumbing to even slight changes in temperature or nutrients.

Since all cells in a plant or an animal are identical genetically, different expressions must be due to plasticity. Cuttings from stems of many fruit-trees can grow into entire trees with stems, roots, flowers, and fruits with characteristics of the plant from which the cuttings were obtained. Corn plants are sufficiently plastic to produce male tassels at the top of the plant and female cobs lower down, all with the same genotype.

Some animals like salamanders and lizards have sufficient plasticity to generate new tails; earthworms can regenerate new heads or new tails. Small pieces of a carrot can be placed in sterile dishes containing nutrients required for cell growth. Individual cells may soon grow and float free in the nutrient solution. From such individual cells, subsequent growth may produce small mounds of cells from which new carrots begin to develop, and which will ultimately grow into mature carrot plants, complete with roots and leaves.

Within a carrot, each cell carries the potential for developing any and all features of an entire carrot plant. Since each carrot cell contains essentially identical genetic potentials, such variable expressions may result from the impact of variable environments. Cells of carrots growing in the ground develop differently than cells above ground. Cells near the surface of a carrot develop differently than cells deep within a tissue.

All living organisms are genetically endowed with sufficient plasticity to provide the variety of expressions elicited by ubiquitous unstable environments. A human nose is composed of cells with the same genetic materials as human tonsils. Cells of a dog's ear are genetically identical to those of its tail. They develop into dramatically different expressions because the environments in which they develop differ.

The cells of every living organism have similar extensive plasticity which permits an array of varied expressions. Each type of God's creatures here on Earth has a tremendous capacity for responding to the many diverse environments that it will encounter during a normal lifetime.

Because of plasticity, when organisms encounter new challenges, the responses may be rather freakish. When insects lay eggs in plant tissues, the new environment often causes a plastic response in which the host plant develops grotesque galls or tumors. Our current unhappy experiences with drug or alcohol consumption by pregnant women demonstrate how human cells are capable of bizarre expressions due to plastic responses in unusual environments. Such practices modify the environments of the developing embryos so much that many newborn infants may be physically or mentally malformed. Of these emerging expressions, it is unlikely that natural selection would identify any that are improvements for survival.

Fortunately, most humans experience almost the same sequence of environments during embryonic development as well as during adult life so that we are each generally equipped with two eyes, one nose, a pair of kidneys, and five digits on each hand. We may well concern ourselves, however, about the effects of novel environments on future generations who may be reared in increasing exposure to polluted air and water, ionizing radiation, pesticides, herbicides, and other toxins including recreational drugs, and perhaps even different stresses present on the moon, Mars, or other planets.

Plasticity is the ability for individual organisms to change attributes in the constantly changing environments they encounter on Earth. Without plasticity, we would have no ears, no noses, no fingers, no hearts. There would be no horses, no trees, no birds. At the subcellular level there would be no mitochondria, no plastids, no endoplasmic reticula. Life as we know it is totally dependent upon phenotypic plasticity. Indeed, all evolution harkens back to plastic responses to environmental changes.

Genetic Flexibility

Flexibility is variation due to genetic variables in populations. Although a carrot cell may have the potential to grow into a carrot root, a leaf, or a flower, it could never, under any known situation, become a radish. Radish cells grow into radishes in the same type of environments in which carrot cells grow into carrots. Much of the variation we see about us is due to genetic flexibility.

Many genetic differences are found in every species on Earth. In humans, genetic differences are responsible for different blood types, differences in skin pigmentation, and differences in stature. There are, in fact, so many genetic differences among human beings that it would be virtually impossible for two individuals to have the same genetic potential.

Since each of us came from the union of two sex-cells, one from each parent, we possess two complete sets of genetic potentials. These two sets are never exactly identical. A person may have received from one parent the genetic potential for forming blue eyes and red hair and, from the other parent, the genes for brown eyes and black hair. A sex-cell from such a person could have the genes for brown eyes and red hair, or brown eyes and black hair, or blue eyes and red hair, or blue eyes and black hair. With just these two variables, four different types of sex-cells are possible. With as few as thirty variables, the potential number of different combinations of sex-cells produced would number in the billions.

The human race is, consequently, extremely genetically variable and the number of possible combinations is nearly infinite. Some of these combinations are worthless and many are lethal, but those that survive are so different from each other that the chances that you or I will ever recur just as we are is astronomically remote. Each of us represents the fruition of a long series of very improbable events. There will never be another Julius Caesar, Thomas S. Monson, Winston Churchill, nor you. Each one of us is guaranteed personal genetic uniqueness.

As noted previously, environmental fluctuations that last less than the lifespan of an individual organism may be accommodated by plasticity; fluctuations extending over longer periods are accommodated by genetic flexibility. Field mice may accommodate environmental changes such as night and day, rain and sunshine, or food and hunger by plastic responses. But lengthy environmental changes such as exposure to new types of predators or changes in available food or changes in the vegetational cover may require genetic-flexibility changes to succeed. Although individuals in a population may not have sufficient plasticity to survive their environmental challenges, populations may escape extinction if they contain sufficient genetic flexibility to expose those individuals which are adaptive.

Most wild rabbits living in north temperate climates plastically change their coat-color from brown to white as the season changes from summer to winter. A genetic change has also been observed among rabbits which have been exposed for many years to a different climatic rhythm. In 1854, one pair of rabbits (*Lepus timidus*) was introduced to the Faroe Islands and, as they were accustomed to do, they rhythmically changed their coat-color from brown to white in periods corresponding to the winter and summer seasons of their native Norway. Their descendants also rhythmically changed coat-color each year from brown to white. However, through the years, some genetic changes accumulated, providing sufficient flexibility to result in some rabbits that remained brown all year. By 1875, only about half the population still turned white in the period corresponding to Norway's winter, and by 1885 this figure had been reduced to only about one fourth. In 1890 hardly any rabbits could be found that turned white and now there are none.[1]

This and other such examples have clearly demonstrated that both plasticity and flexibility are controlled genetically and can be altered by selection. Most plastic responses are advantageous under the circumstances in which an organism lives. But a change in the environment might favor a different genetic background which provides a better plastic response. As new challenges arise, so will new varieties and races and species.

Each new species which thus comes forth must, to be success-ful, be sufficiently plastic to adjust to the routine fluctuations which occur during the lifetime of individuals and also be suffi-ciently flexible to yield new genetic combinations, some of which may be improvements.

One of the greatest gifts that God has furnished His chil-dren is the gift of free agency. In many respects the vast array of possible phenotypic choices of plants and animals is comparable to the free agency that God gives all of His children. The infinite variety of habitats on Earth and nearly infinite variety of proto-plasmic expressions which occupy those habitats were prerequi-site for the creation of life on Earth and for the host of adapted organisms which have come forth from them. It is a wonderful display of biological free-agency provided by God from the beginning. This attribute was not only required for existence but also requisite for eternal progression into the future.

From these great interactions have come forth the numer-ous successful species which now inhabit the Earth. The drama is succinctly summarized in Genesis 1:11: "Let the earth bring forth . . . the fruit tree yielding fruit after his kind." The com-mand, "Let the earth bring forth," declares that God has cre-ated the Earth and is now allowing the Earth to fulfill its des-tiny. This phrase from the Bible beautifully expresses what scientists describe as the process of organic evolution.

Given sufficient plasticity and flexibility, grass and fruit trees and herbs and cattle and "creeping things" are being con-tinually generated from the Earth. Given sufficient genetic sta-bility, they "yield fruit" after their own kind. Without sufficient variation—or genetic free-agency—they cannot come forth and without sufficient plasticity they cannot continue. All plants, ani-mals, and microbes that grace our beautiful planet are wonder-fully adapted to their environments but are somewhat less than perfect and somewhat more than chaotic. Moderation in all things is truly a basic biological virtue, a prerequisite for life.

Plasticity and flexibility are both controlled genetically providing further evidence that a sudden special creation would not have been the source of the numerous species of plants and animals which have come forth from the Earth.

Since it is impossible for any organism or biological attribute to exist without plasticity, every biological attribute began as a plastic response to some environmental assault. Consequently all organic evolution is ultimately derived from plastic responses to novel environments. An environmentally induced attribute, reinforced by genetic modifiers can subsequently become genetically independent, a process described as genetic assimilation by geneticist Conrad H. Waddington.[2]

What a marvelous plan God has provided! "In the beginning" (Gen. 1:1), plants and animals began on Earth as simple plastic responses to their ever-changing environments. As these simple responses became redundant, predictability became more secure. Repetitive responses could be predicted, and random novel responses were replaced by highly predictable ones. The Lord's words, "Let us prepare the earth to bring forth" (Abr. 4:11) was made comprehensible. Every plant and animal verifies that this has indeed been accomplished. It is the crowning response in evolution and a primary message of the holy scriptures.

Notes

1. L. G. Ingles, *Mammals of the Pacific States: California, Oregon, and Washington* (Stanford, Calif., Stanford University Press, 1965).

2. Conrad H. Waddington, "Genetic Assimilation of an Acquired Character," *Evolution* 7 (1953): 118–26.

2
New Species from Mutations

Today there are more than five million species of plants and animals on the Earth and thousands of additional species are being discovered each year.[1] According to the scriptural accounts, these all came forth from the Earth as planned in the beginning.

> And God said, Let the earth bring forth grass. (Gen. 1:11)
> And the Gods said: Let us prepare the earth to bring forth grass. . . .
> And the Gods organized the earth to bring forth grass. (Abr. 4:11–12)

Ever since the Earth was created, many new species have come forth and others have become extinct. After decades of scientific study, evidence has accumulated that these have all been derived by means of organic evolution. This process is also harmonious with the scriptural account, "Let the earth bring forth."

Numerous scientific studies have established that the Earth brings forth new species by three methods: (1) accumulation of mutations, (2), sexual recombination, and especially among plants (3) polyploidy. These three processes are not mutually exclusive in nature, and many species arise as the result of combinations among them. None is effective without isolation, either reproductive or environmental. All three avenues for speciation are important in the evolution of plants, but most species of animals are derived only from accumulations of gene mutations and chromosome rearrangements. Only a few animal species have been derived from interspecific sexual recombination and only a few have been derived by polyploidy.

Mutations have been widely studied by scientists for decades. In a small nursery at Brigham Young University, Provo, Utah, a study was made of cultivated rye and its relatives.[2] Over the course of time, a number of new mutations appeared. Some caused very little change in appearance, but some changed the plants so much that they no longer resembled rye. One mutation affected the number of spikelets produced at each node in rye heads. Instead of a single floret, as many as four were formed. This mutation altered the plant's appearance so much that when it first appeared in the nursery it was nearly discarded as a weed. Because it had multiple spikelets it was named *Secale cereale* variety *elymoides*. It was because of plasticity that some nodes produced one floret, some two, some three, and some four. By selection it was possible to obtain pure-bred lines in which all plants had the same number of florets at each node and also lines in which the number of florets per node varied within individuals. Other mutations also appeared during this study. Some mutant rye plants grew prostrate on the ground, others erect like a bush. Some had branching stems, some had branching heads, and some had multiple heads. Some had fragile heads, while others were stiff. The seeds were also different: long, round, short, or shriveled. The leaves could be long, lax and broad, short and stiff, or narrow and curled.

Almost every living species which has been examined critically has shown a similar propensity for acquiring new mutations. The tiny fruit fly, which has been examined about as closely as any organism on Earth, has manifested mutations affecting nearly every part of its body. One mutation changed antennae into legs. Another provided four wings instead of two. Another caused the flies to respond differently to gravity. One study found thirty-two different mutations among just 239 fruit flies collected in nature.[3]

Decades ago, DDT was widely used as a pesticide. As a result, DDT-resistant mosquitoes emerged, because any mutant mosquito that resisted DDT had an advantage over DDT-susceptible mosquitoes. In areas treated with DDT, the populations quickly shifted to resistant forms, rendering DDT ineffective for mosquito control.

Similarly, certain antibiotics, such as penicillin, were once considered miracle cures for a wide variety of illnesses caused by bacteria. When prescribed by a physician, these antibiotics effectively killed disease-causing bacteria that had infected people. Many bacterial diseases, such as cholera and tuberculosis, were nearly eradicated in parts of the world where antibiotics were readily available. However, bacteria resistant to once-effective antibiotics have emerged in recent years because the widespread use of these antibiotics has favored the survival and reproduction of resistant bacteria. Physicians responded by administering more than one antibiotic at a time to increase the chances of killing drug-resistant bacteria. In response, multi-drug resistant bacteria emerged, which must be treated with powerful new antibiotics. And bacteria resisant to these new antibiotics are now appearing.

Mutations also affect many characteristics among humans, including blood proteins, fertility, longevity, intelligence, and even temperament. Each one of us carries numerous mutant genes which remain unexpressed because they are recessive and carried only in a single dose. Many would cause death if they occurred homozygously (in double dose).

Most new mutations, in all organisms, are both recessive and harmful. These attributes are very significant in determining the role of mutations in the origin of species. Since the majority of new mutations are harmful, they are eventually discarded. However, because they are also usually recessive, they may persist for many generations before being entirely eliminated.

Therefore, sexual populations that can keep mutations around until they have an opportunity to be associated with other gene combinations may give rise to new valuable traits. This characteristic may be the principal value of the recessive nature of new mutations, established by natural selection. Because harmful dominant attributes will be eliminated as they occur, the remaining dominant traits tend to be non-harmful.

Most natural populations appear to be quite stable generation after generation as expressed in the biblical account: "And out of the ground the Lord God formed every beast of the field and every fowl of the air; and brought them unto Adam to see what he would call them: and whatsoever Adam called every living creature, that was the name thereof" (Gen. 2:19).

Most sexual species are loaded with stores of mutations that are shuffled and reshuffled at each sexual cycle. Usually successful organisms will be those which most resemble their successful parents. However, as new environments become available, other characteristics may succeed.

This pattern has been dramatically illustrated in historical times in species which can exploit new environments because of human activities. In the St. Lawrence Valley in North America, for instance, many new species of wild hawthorns (*Crataegus*) have come into existence after colonists cleared heavily forested areas and opened them up for agriculture. In 1848 only seven species of hawthorns were known in the eastern United States, but by 1907 sixty-five species were described.[4]

This phenomenal eruption of new hawthorn species probably involved the interplay of several evolutionary forces but apparently sprang primarily from the vast store of variables that had already accumulated as recessive mutations. The combinations which proved most successful for the new habitats had undoubtedly appeared repeatedly in earlier periods; but until the forests were cleared, the environment was not suitable for them to flourish and reproduce successfully. The value of such stores of mutations in speciation is profound, emerging when new environments are made available.

Selection experiments conducted with corn at the Illinois Experimental Station at the University of Illinois since the 1890s to select for increased protein content have shown a steady increase in protein for many years. This has been possible because of the many available gene combinations for increased protein content in corn.[5] Similarly, a selection experiment in mice indicated that there must have already been at least 100–300 genetic variables available in mice to permit the extensive variation in growth rate revealed by twenty-five generations of selection.[6]

As these examples illustrate, mice, corn, humans, flies, and hawthorns—and all other forms of life on Earth—constantly acquire new mutations.

Wild beets (*Beta maritima*) growing on European seashores have accumulated enough new genetic variables in historical times to permit the selection of at least four distinct valuable species: garden beets, sugarbeets, chard, and mangels. Wild beets were domesticated as a source of greens but later selection for forms with swollen underground stems led to the development of mangels as an excellent source of cattle-feed. Red forms, high in sugar-content, led to the development of the common garden beet about four hundred years ago. A Prussian plant breeder by the name of Franz Karl Achard began intensive selection for high sugar content in beets early in the nineteenth century, resulting in the development of the sugar beet. They have been grown in the United States only since 1875.[7] What a marvelous product from a wild unpalatable ancestor!

Horses have accumulated enough mutations to produce huge Percherons, fleet thoroughbreds, and tiny Shetlands.

Two species of wild snapdragons have accumulated so many mutations that, among thousands of descendants from a cross between two of them, not a single plant was found that could be identified as the same as one of the parents.[8]

Some characteristics tend to disintegrate and disappear as a result of selection. Animals in lightless caves are often blind simply because there are more ways of being blind than of not being blind. Unless alternatives to the formation of functional eyes are discarded, the probability of having those particular attributes that produce functional eyes is so small that, given enough time, blindness is not uncommon. Such blind species include salamanders, lizards, fish, and even marsupial moles in Australia.

With such an extensive array of genetic variation available to most species on Earth, new species can and do arise from their genetic pools. Even in the absence of other avenues for speciation, incessantly, day after day and generation after generation, new mutations accumulate. As they are shuffled and reshuffled in each reproductive cycle, they provide the opportunity for an ever richer array of species to give beauty and variety to the Earth. Genetic variables provide what may be called the "biological free-agency" prerequisite for refinement and progression.

"And the Gods said: Let us prepare the earth to bring forth . . . " (Abr. 4:11).

Notes

1. Society for Conservation Biology, "Just How Many Species Are There, Anyway?" *ScienceDaily*, May 26, 2003.

2. H. C. Stutz, (1962) "Within-Penetrance, between Penetrance and Expressivity: Of the Elymoides Mutant in Rye," *Journal of Heredity* 53, no. 2 (1962): 66–71.

3. Thomas Hunt Morgan, *Contributions to the Genetics of Drosophila Melanogaster*, with A. H. Sturtevant and C. B. Bridges (Washington, D.C.: Carnegie Institution of Washington, 1919).

4. Arnold Arboretum, *Bulletin of Popular Information*, No. 42 (Jamaica Plain, Mass.: Arnold Arboretum, Harvard University, 1913).

5. M. Bjarnason and S. K. Vasal, "Breeding of Quality Protein Maize (QPM)," in *Plant Breeding Reviews*, edited by J. Janick (New York: John Wiley & Sons, 1992), 9:181–216.

6. P. D. Keightley and W. G. Hill, "Quantitative Genetic Variation in Body Size of Mice from New Mutations," *Genetics* 131, no. 3 (1992): 693–700.

7. G. K. G. Campbell, Sugar "Beet," *Evolution of Crop Plants*, edited by N. W. Simmonds. (New York: Longman, 1976), 25–28.

8. Z. Schwarz-Sommer, B. Davies, et al. (2003). "An Everlasting Pioneer: The Story of Antirrhinum Research," *National Review of Genetics* 4, no. 8 (2003): 657-66.

3
New Species from Sexual Recombination

Although the definition of a species is often controversial, conceptually each species identifies populations that are sufficiently separated from their associates either morphologically or reproductively to be considered unique. Among the definitions of species which have been used profitably by researchers is one that refers to populations which are evolutionarily distinct. This definition usually includes reproductive isolation, either genetically (due to flexibility) or environmentally (due to plasticity).

Although new species can arise from accumulations of new mutations, the amount of genetic variation available for speciation among plants is often dramatically increased by interspecific sexual hybridization. Well-documented examples of this process are provided by studies of many species including some common range-plants of the Intermountain West.

A conspicuous example is displayed by hybrids between *Purshia tridentata* (bitterbrush), an important wildland forage shrub, and *Cowania stansburyana* (cliffrose), a small, related, but unpalatable rangeland tree. Bitterbrush grows on lower mountain slopes in Utah, Idaho, Nevada, California, Oregon, and Washington. Throughout the entire state of Utah, it is often in contact with and hybridizes with its distant relative, cliffrose, which grows throughout Utah and Arizona, and south into Mexico. Bitterbrush and cliffrose are so different that taxonomists consider them distinct genera. Throughout Utah, they hybridize so freely that it has not been possible to find a population of bitterbrush completely free of plants showing *Cowania* characteristics. From these hybrids have come a wide variety of plants showing nearly every conceivable combination of the traits of the two parents. Most of these combinations are probably worthless, but many survive and some appear to be more adaptive than the parental combinations.

South of Utah, some of the new combinations have permitted modified bitterbrush to extend into the drier, hotter regions of Arizona and New Mexico. Among these new, successful combinations is a new species that now reproduces independently in these desert hills. Taxonomically it is known as *Purshia glandulosa* (glandular bitterbrush). It has several distinct attributes of both parents, including the profuse presence of glands on the leaves found in cliffrose but not in bitterbrush, and three parted leaf tips as in bitterbrush but not in cliffrose.[1]

Although cliffrose does not grow north of Utah, nearly all populations of bitterbrush throughout Idaho, Washington, and Oregon have conspicuous cliffrose attributes. Many of these new combinations appear to be superior to normal bitterbrush in the northern latitudes. Because they are less palatable to sheep, they are preferentially spared under heavy grazing. Consequently, a new species appears to be emerging in these more northern areas due to the new environments created by domesticated sheep.

Cultivated strawberries also originated from interspecific hybridization between distantly related species. In 1714 a French spy brought to France five plants of wild strawberries (*Fragaria chiloensis*) from southern Chile. He nourished them for six months aboard ship during the journey to Europe and placed them in a nursery in France. Also growing in this nursery were plants of a wild strawberry from eastern North America (*Fragaria virginiana*). The fruits of the Chilean strawberry are much larger than the wild strawberries of eastern North America but have a rather poor flavor—"very little superior in flavor to the potato," according to an English gourmet, William

Corbett.[2] All five South American plants were female and so required cross-pollination to set fruit, a process accomplished by hybridizing with the male strawberries from North America. This hybrid plant was hermaphroditic (both male and female flowers on the same plant) and fertile. From this hybrid and similar hybrids came many new combinations among which nearly all varieties of modern strawberries have been derived.[3] What a wonderful product from such an unusual union!

Almost every modern domesticated animal and many plants have been derived from products of sexual recombination. Some of the contacts are hidden in antiquity, but many of them have occurred within historical times, and some even within the last few years. Modern sugarcane varieties were derived from hybridization between cultivated sugarcane (*Saccharum officinarum*) and a related wild grass species (*Saccharum spontaneum*).

Several years ago a new breed of cattle (*Santa gertrudis*) was introduced in southern Texas. It was deliberately synthesized from hybrids between Indian cattle (*Bos indicus*) and the common shorthorn cattle of America (*Bos taurus*) to provide a high quality beef-producer which could tolerate the climatic and range conditions of southern Texas.[4]

This avenue of speciation is so successful and so rapid, particularly among plants, that we not only have numerous documented examples of new species that have originated in nature within historical times, but we have also been able to use hybridization to artificially synthesize new species and to introduce new characteristics into existing species as a fruitful basis for improvement.

The sudden appearance of some hybrids and hybrid products may superficially appear to be supportive of the tenets of "creationism." However, since interspecific sexual recombination would have required the involvement of separate multiple events, they are much more likely to be products of natural selection.

Notes

1. H. C. Stutz and L. K. Thomas, "Hybridization and Introgression in Cowania and Pushia," *Evolution* 18 (1964): 183–98.

2. William Corbett, quoted in S. W. Fletcher, *The Strawberry in North America* (New York: 1917), 116.

3. G. M. Darrow, *The Strawberry: History, Breeding and Physiology*, New England Institute for Medical Research (New York: Holt, Rinehart and Winston, 1966).

4. H. M. Briggs and D. M. Briggs, *Modern Breeds of Livestock* (New York: MacMillan, 1980).

4
Speciation in Plants by Polyploidy

Another way that the Earth has brought forth new species is observed in the study of chromosomes. Characteristics that distinguish species from each other are ultimately derived from changes in DNA within chromosomes. Many plant species also have distinguishing differences resulting from duplications of whole sets of chromosomes.

Most animals, including humans, have two sets of chromosomes in each cell (one set from each parent). Many plant species, however are polyploid (poly = many, ploid = fold). Polyploid species have multiple sets of chromosomes in their cells. Diploid species have two sets, tetraploid species have four sets, hexaploid species have six sets, octoploids have eight sets, etc. The increase in the number of sets of chromosomes in plants is often phenomenal. Ferns, for instance, may have more than a thousand chromosomes.

More than half of all flowering plants on earth today originated as polyploids. Polyploid species occur commonly in plants and less frequently in animals. Most polyploids are derived from simple errors during cell division. There are two types of polyploids: autopolyploids and allopolyploids. Failure of the mitotic spindle to separate *chromatids* during anaphase of *mitosis* results directly in the formation of autopolyploid cells with double the usual number of chromosomes. Failure to separate homologous *chromosomes* during first anaphase of *meiosis* may lead to the formation of cells having an unreduced number of chromosomes. Sex-cells derived from this aberration may function in the formation of allopolyploidy.

Autopolyploids

Since autopolyploid plants consist of cells containing identical multiple sets of chromosomes, they seldom contain much genetic flexibility, nor do they express much heterosis (hybrid vigor.) Consequently they usually succeed best in uniform environments.

Because agriculturalists usually deliberately try to provide uniform environments for their crops, many agricultural crops—including potatoes, alfalfa, raspberries, and some forms of orchard grass—are autopolyploids. Autopolyploid rangeland species usually occur as sizeable uniform dense populations, occupying well-defined uniform environments.

An example of the successful origin and establishment of an autopolyploid species in nature is provided by shadscale (*Atriplex confertifolia*), an important range plant in the western United States.[1] The uniform environment required for the successful origin and establishment of this autopolyploid occurs in the uniform valleys and lower slopes of the former Lake Bonneville. For thousands of years, the lake precluded the presence of vegetation. About ten to twelve thousand years ago, Lake Bonneville broke out at Redrock Pass and drained into the Snake River, lowering the lake level about 250 feet. Subsequently, what must have been a horrendous drought dried up most of the remaining Lake Bonneville as evidenced by conspicuous shorelines throughout most of Utah and Nevada. Vast areas of uniform landscapes were exposed, ideal for the invasion of neighboring plant species and the origin and establishment of new uniform species, including new polyploids.

Above the upper lake terraces of Lake Bonneville, current populations of shadscale plants are diploid. They contain considerable genetic variation affecting traits such as flowering-time, leaf dimensions, and stature. Below the lake-level terraces, current populations of shadscales are polyploid. They occur in dense, uniform populations and show very little between-plant variation. Some populations extend for many miles. Phenotypic differences between populations suggest multiple, separate origins.[2] Considering the ease with which new autopolyploid species may emerge, the origin of new polyploid populations is likely a clear portrayal of the Earth "bringing forth" new species to occupy new environments.

Autopolyploids usually closely resemble their diploid parents but some express distinct differences. In Juab County, Utah, a distinctive diploid form of fourwing saltbush (*Atriplex canescens gigantea*) appears in the extensive sand dunes northwest of Lynndyl. This plant has large fourwinged fruits and often grows to a height of more than eight feet. The giant diploids are confined to the sand dunes themselves while the fourwing tetraploids grow only on the sandy soils surrounding the dunes. The contrasting soil differences result in severe isolation of the two species, reinforced by an effective reproduction barrier: the diploids flower five or six weeks later than the tetraploids.[3]

In southern New Mexico chromosome races of fourwing saltbush are also isolated by edaphic (soil) differences. Diploids grow only on the sand dunes as they do in Utah, tetraploids grow only on sandy soils, and hexaploids are confined to heavy clay soils.[4]

Since the distribution of the chromosome races of *Atriplex canescens* is closely correlated in this instance with environmental differences, the evolutionary history of *Atriplex canescens* is clearly harmonious with its origin by organic evolution rather than by special creation.

"And the earth brought forth grass, and herb yielding seed after his kind, and the tree yielding fruit whose seed was in itself, after his kind: and God saw that it was good" (Gen. 1:12).

Allopolyploids

Many well-known cultivated plant species—including wheat, cotton, and rutabaga—are allopolyploids. Each allopolyploid species is derived directly from a sterile hybrid between two species. Because such hybrids contain only one set of chromosomes from each parent, their chromosomes are incapable of normal synapses (pairing of homologous chromosomes) in meiosis and are therefore sterile. But when an aberration during meiosis occurs in which chromosomes fail to separate at first anaphase, the result is the doubling of the chromosome sets. Each chromosome is provided with an exact replica with which it can synapse in later meiotic divisions. The resulting allopolyploid cells have two of every chromosome and therefore can have normal meiosis and full fertility. They are initially homozygous for every attribute and thus may become well-defined allopolyploid species. Speciation by allopolyploidy is so dramatic in nature that it is oftimes described as "quantum speciation."

Triticale, an economically valuable crop-plant derived from the hybrid between wheat (*Triticum*) and rye (*Secale*), is a typical allopolyploid species and is easily produced experimentally. Wheat is a hexaploid species with six sets of chromosomes (AABBCC). Rye is diploid, with two sets (DD). Sex-cells (gametes) of wheat have three sets and sex cells of rye have one set. Wheat × rye hybrids therefore have 3 + 1 = 4 sets (ABCD). Both wheat and rye have seven chromosomes in each set; but because the chromosomes of wheat are unlike rye chromosomes, both in number and in genetic content, the chromosomes of wheat × rye hybrids cannot pair up in meiosis and the hybrid plants are sterile. However, plant breeders may treat the wheat × rye hybrid plants with a chemical called colchicine, which causes the chromosomes to duplicate themselves without cell division. The treated cells then have two sets of both wheat and rye chromosomes, and the resulting plants are fully fertile. This fertile allopolyploid is Triticale, a specialized grain with limited commercial value.[5]

The meiotic error is sufficiently common in hybrid plants to have been responsible for the origin of many allopolyploid species. In the laboratory, the necessary meiotic error can be promoted with a variety of shocks applied to the growing points (meristems) of such sterile interspecific hybrids to deliberately produce synthetic allopolyploid species. One of the most effective treatments in the laboratory to induce polyploidy is the application of colchicine, a chemical derived from plants of the genus *Colchicum*. When applied to growing points, colchicine promotes errors in dividing cells. Several new species have been "created" using this technique. Synthetic allopolyploid species of native grasses are particularly easy to generate, and several have been developed at Utah State University, including a few that have proven to be agronomically useful.[6]

Cultivated cotton (*Gossypium hirsutum*) is another allopolyploid species whose origin is known. Its parents are *Gossypium arboreum*, an Old World cultivated diploid species with thirteen pairs of large chromosomes, and *Gossypium raimondii*, a New World, wild, lintless diploid species with thirteen pairs of small chromosomes.[7] Hybrids between them are sterile with thirteen large chromosomes and thirteen small chromosomes. The number of chromosomes in the hybrids can be doubled, creating synthetic allopolyploid plants that closely resemble native *Gossypium hirsutum*. They are fertile and produce copious amounts of lint. *Gossypium hirsutum* created in a laboratory is so much like cultivated *Gossypium hirsutum* that the species' origin in nature must have occurred very recently. If it had occurred anciently, new mutations would, expectedly, have modified both parents as well as the polyploid derivative.[8]

Other well-known cultivated allopolyploid species include rutabaga derived from turnip × cabbage hybrids,[9] Raphanobrassica (radish × cabbage)[10] and wheat (*Triticum × Aegilops*).[11]

The evidence of the abundant polyploidy species in nature and the synthesis in the laboratory of cultivated cotton and other polyploids argues against their origin by special creation. Rather, it provides evidence that the Earth continually brings forth new species through the process of organic evolution as planned in the beginning.

As these examples have shown, the processes by which species originate are now quite well understood. Have these same processes been responsible for the origin of all species on earth? Most biologists agree that the evidence strongly supports such a conclusion. The next six chapters summarize the principal evidences supporting the theory of speciation by evolution: the fossil record, geographical and ecological distribution patterns, embryology, anatomical evidence, biochemical patterns, and genetics.

Notes

1. H. C. Stutz, "Chromosome Races of *Atriplex confertifolia*," *Proceedings of the Society of Range Management* (1978).

2. H. C. Stutz and S. C. Sanderson, "Evolutionary Studies of *Atriplex*: Chromosome Races of *A. confertifolia* (Shadscale)," *American Journal of Botany* 77 (1983): 490–98.

3. H. C. Stutz, J. M. Melby, and G. K. Livingston, "Evolutionary Studies of *Atriplex*: A Relic *gigas* Diploid Population of *Atriplex canescens*," *American Journal of Botany* 62 (1975): 236–45.

4. Max P. Dunford, "Cytotype Distribution of *Atriplex canescens* (*Chenopodiaceae*) of Southern New Mexico and Adjacent Texas," *Southwestern Naturalist* 29, no. 2 (1984): 223–28.

5. E. A. Oelke, E. S. Oplinger, et al., *Triticale: Alternative Field Crops Manual* (Madison: University of Wisconsin Extension Service, 2002).

6. Shafqat Farooq and Farooqe Azam, "A New Allopolyploid Wheat for Stressed Lands and Poverty Alleviation," *Field Crops Research* 100, nos. 2–3 (February 1, 2007): 369–73.

7. Y. P. S. Bijaj, "Cotton," *Biotechnology in Agriculture and Forestry* (New York: Springer-Verlag, 1998), 3–36.

8. L. L. Phillips, "Cotton," in *Evolution of Crop Plants*, edited by N. W. Simmonds (New York: Longman, 1976).

9. H. Namai and T. Hosoda, (1967). "On Breeding of Brassica Napus Obtained from Artificially Induced Amphidiploids: III On the Breeding of Synthetic Rutabaga (B. napus var rapifera)," *Japanese Journal of Breeding* 17 (1967): 78–148.

10. G. D. Karpechenko, "Polyploid Hybrids of *Raphanus sativus L.* X *Brassica oleracea L.*," *Zeitschrift fur inductive Abstammungs- und Vererbungslehre* 48 (1928): 1–85.

11. M. Feldman, "Wheats," *Evolution of Crop Plants*, edited by N. W. Simmonds (New York: Longman, 1976).

5

The Fossil Record

In many places throughout the world, sedimentary rocks contain fossils of organisms that once lived in that locale. Unfortunately the fossil record is meager—incomplete, fragmentary, and discontinuous. But because it is the only documented history that we have of ancient life, it is priceless.

The opportunity for an organism to be represented as a fossil is so slim that it is really a marvel that we have as many fossil records as we do. Considering the demanding requirements for fossilization, the unusual circumstances under which fossilization occurs, the multitude of destructive forces which eradicate fossils even after they are formed, the remote possibility that a fossil will be found, and the unlikelihood that a fossil which is found will ever reach the hands of someone who can interpret its story, it is remarkable indeed that the fossil record is as meaningful as it is.

Fossils are formed under very specific circumstances with the result that only a small number of plants and animals are ever preserved. To become fossilized, an organism must become quickly buried in an anaerobic grave before decomposition can destroy it. This requirement usually means a catastrophic accident such as being buried by a flash flood, mudslide, or volcanic ash, or by perishing in deep lakes or seas. Consequently, plants and animals living near or in rivers, lakes, or seas are more likely to become preserved as fossils than those on land. Also, since predominantly hard body-parts such as bone or wood lend themselves to fossilization, it is rare to find much detail preserved in a fossilized soft-tissued specimen.

Yet in spite of the extreme unlikelihood that any particular organism will become fossilized, because of the long time since plants and animals first appeared on earth, many have been preserved. Although only a small fraction of them have been discovered, with each new excavation or exposed outcropping, the museums accumulate more and more of these exciting documents.

When layers of sedimentary rock are brought into view as outcroppings or as canyon cliffs, they often appear as huge, stony books of documented history. The lower layers contain fossils of more ancient organisms; fossils in upper layers resemble more recent organisms.

Many methods have been used to determine the age of fossils. One of the most reliable methods comes from radioactive "clocks." Since the rate of decomposition is remarkably constant for each radioactive element, changes in the amount of a radioactive isotope in a specimen provide a reliable index of the specimen's age.

Relatively recent events can be quite accurately dated by the use of radioactive carbon (^{14}C). In today's atmosphere, most carbon has an atomic mass of 12 and is symbolized as ^{12}C; but due to bombardment by high-energy particles from space, a small amount of nitrogen (^{14}N) in the atmosphere is converted to radioactive carbon (^{14}C). As plants take up carbon dioxide in photosynthesis, some of it will be radioactive ^{14}C. This radioactive element is distributed throughout the plant in the same proportion that it exists in the atmosphere. Since animals obtain their carbon ultimately from plants, they too contain radioactive ^{14}C in the same proportion as it appears in the plants and in the atmosphere.

After death, plants and animals take in no more carbon, but the radioactive ^{14}C present in their tissues continues to decompose to ^{14}N. It takes about 5,730 years for half of any quantity of ^{14}C to be degraded to ^{14}N. Consequently, by determining the relative proportions of ^{12}C and ^{14}C in a specimen, a rather accurate estimate of its age can be calculated.

Older rocks are dated by measuring the radioactive decay of elements which decompose more slowly than ^{14}C. For instance, it requires about 4.5 billion years for half of a quantity of uranium 238 to decompose to lead 206. The half-life of beryllium 10 is about 1.36 million years and the half-life of potassium 40 is about 1.3 billion years.

By studying these slowly decaying radioactive elements, scientists have estimated the age of some fossil-bearing rocks at more than three billion years. Some meteorites have been estimated to have an age of about 4.5 billion years. Since such meteorites may be the same age as the Earth, the commonly accepted conclusion from such research is that the Earth is about 4.5 billion years old.

Except for evidence of fossil remains for simple single-celled plants and animals and some bacteria-like organisms, the most ancient macroscopic fossil record extends back only somewhat more than 600 million years.

The first land-animals and land-plants appear in the fossil record about 400 million years ago. Many large groups flourished for a short time but later became extinct. Some appear to be the ancestors of modern plants and animals. Others appear to have left no descendants. Coal beds, for instance, are made largely of giant "horse-tails" (*equisteum*), club mosses, and ferns, which produced extensive populations but which have since become almost extinct.

Gymnosperms and reptiles thrived for more than two hundred million years. When the gymnosperms began to decline and flowering plants replaced them, insects, birds, and mammals also flourished. There is some evidence that the great variety of insects and the great variety of flowering plants arose simultaneously with each contributing to the success of the other.

More recent geological history is much more easily interpreted so our information about population changes during the past one or two million years is quite extensive. Not only are there petrified fossils as informative clues but there are actual remains in caves, tar pits, and peat bogs. In some places, telltale evidences of former lakes, glaciers, floods, and deserts are still well preserved.

All of these fossil evidences support the interpretation that the formation and demise of the myriad of species of plants and animals required a very long period of time. However, the creationists' hypothesis argues that their formation would have been a more sudden and recent occurrence, a view that conflicts with much of what is demonstrated in the fossil record.

Fossils contained in sedimentary rocks in western North America, dating to 150-200 million years ago, indicate that many tropical and subtropical plants flourished in this area during that time. Fossils of palms, sequoias, ginkgos, araucarias, magnolias, figs, cinnamons, walnuts, and ferns indicate that, prior to the uplift of the Rocky Mountains, this area had a warm, humid climate. At that time, Greenland apparently had about the same climate. Fossils of these same kinds of plants have been found in Greenland in rocks of about the same age.

In central North America, a great fluctuating sea covered most of Utah and Colorado. With the uplift of the Mesocordilleran geosyncline, rivers flowed eastward. It was in some of the great floods of this time that numerous dinosaurs became preserved in great abundance. Associated with them were cycads, pines, other conifers, and in some areas even palms. It was at this time or shortly afterward that dinosaurs became extinct. Mammals and birds began to appear more commonly in the fossil record and eventually spread throughout the entire world.

Even more significant than the existence of fossils as evidence for evolutionary changes are the apparent differences in rates of evolution among ancient species. If each rock stratum contained fossils of plants and animals—all of which were discrete and distinct from those of other strata—it might be possible to argue, as some have, that fossils represent relics of lifeforms transported to Earth from other planets. But the fossil record is replete with examples of some organisms that exhibit very rapid change from one period to another, yet are preserved along with other species which have changed very little. For instance, the fossil record of opossums shows that, during the past eighty million years, they have remained almost unchanged, while during the same period at least eight different genera of horses have come and gone. Crocodiles have changed very little during the past 125 million years. But in the same strata that display a monotonously uniform history of crocodiles and opossums, other groups are represented by an array of rapidly changing forms. Just since the end of the Cretaceous period (65 million years ago) the fossil record indicates that several major groups of mammals have come into existence.

The fossil record depicting the evolutionary history of the horse is unusually complete—much more so than for most other organisms which have been studied. In the same rocks which have recorded a rapid evolution of horses, the fossil record of ancestors of some other forms of life appear remarkably uniform and similar to those living on earth today. Ginkgo trees, for instance, appear to be about the same today as they were 150 million years ago.

Many species which were anciently abundant are now extinct or are greatly reduced in numbers. The lush forests of giant horsetails, common on earth during the time that the great coal beds were forming, are gone; seed-ferns are extinct. Luxuriant meadows of *Psilophyta*, common 300 million years ago, are represented today by only a few plants belonging to two genera of a single family. Many genera of club-mosses adorned the earth 200 million years ago. Today only a few rare representatives remain. All dinosaurs, ichthyosaurs, and pleiosaurs are gone.

Such disparity in the origin of different groups of organisms through time minimizes the possibility of special creation but accentuates the validity of speciation by evolution. Whereas special creation would have yielded little variation within each taxonomic group, the ongoing evolutionary forces reflect the environmental changes which have occurred and are still occurring throughout time. The command to "let the earth bring forth" appears to have been accomplished and is still being accomplished by biological speciation.

The lengthy time required for the evolutionary changes depicted by fossils is also portrayed by the enormous magnitude of some of the accumulated sedimentary deposits. Studies of subterranean deposits below the floor of the Mediterranean Sea reveal the presence of salt deposits more than 600 meters thick. In south-central Utah are salt deposits more than a mile thick. Exposed sandstone formations thousands of feet thick and massive limestone mountains all testify of very long periods of deposition. It becomes evident that our planet is very, very old—old enough to have accumulated massive deposits of sedimentary rocks and significant representative fossils of organisms that flourished and evolved through hundreds of millions of years.

Whether their dating is precisely accurate or whether the recorded sequences are perfect or whether the interpretation of ancestry is true, the fossil record is there. It cannot and should not be ignored. It is our only concrete document of ancient history. The theory of speciation by evolution offers a clear, logical explanation for the origin of the fossils and how they relate to the plants and animals now living on earth. Alternative explanations are not equally satisfactory, and they lack supporting evidences, either scriptural or scientific. Consequently most biologists accept the theory of speciation by evolution as the most likely correct explanation. It not only adequately accounts for the sequential modifications of plants and animals that chronologically came to resemble the species now living on earth, but it also accounts for and even requires the extensive time involved in the accumulation of the fossil record.

6
Distribution Patterns as Evidence for Evolution

When a particular kind of plant or animal is found in nature in only one place on Earth, it is referred to as being endemic to that place. Eucalyptus trees are endemic to Australia. Giant redwood trees are endemic to California. Giraffes and hippopotamuses are endemic to Africa. Many other species enjoy a much wider distribution, and some are even circumglobal. Polar bears are circumpolar in northern continents. Junipers are found in the mountains of North America, Europe, and Asia.

Endemic species are present on every continent and most islands of the world, but they are far more abundant in the continents of the southern hemisphere than in the north. Only in Australia are there kangaroos, wombats, and koalas. Except for the opossums of North America and the marsupial rats of South America, Australia is the only place in the world where there are pouched mammals (marsupials). The absence of other common species such as horses, cows, dogs, cats, elephants, giraffes, tomatoes, cucumbers, pine trees, sagebrush, and bananas is just as striking.

New Zealand lacks any native mammals except for two species of bats. It has no native snake species nor any amphibians except for four species of frog. The tuatara is an entire endemic order of reptile native only to New Zealand. Africa is renowned for its peculiar array of jungle plants and animals—

rhinoceroses, ostriches, gorillas, chimpanzees, baboons, leopards and lions (but, contrary to Hollywood scriptwriters, no tigers), giraffes, zebras, watermelon, coffee, and sorghum.

South American and Central American endemics include anteaters, sloths, boa constrictors, yaks, llamas, corn, beans, cocoa, tomatoes, potatoes, and peppers. Among the endemics of India are Bengal tigers, horned rhinoceroses, bananas, and eggplants. In fact, fully 30 percent of the world's recorded flora is endemic to India.

Northern hemispheric continents also contain many endemics but they are much less common than on the continents of the southern hemisphere. Apparently the southern hemispheric oceans provided greater isolation, and many organisms evolved there exclusively.

Northern hemispheric continents—including North America, Europe, and Asia—all have in common many representative species of pines, firs, spruces, larches, elms, oaks, raspberries, walnuts, hazelnuts, willows, and apples. The moose of North America are very similar to the elk of northern Europe and Asia. Bears, wolves, weasels, and rabbits are circumpolar.

New Zealand has been an isolated island since long before there were mammals on Earth; and because mammals have been unable to cross the formidable seawater barrier which lies between the continents on which they originated and New Zealand, none are present on that island.

Australia appears to have been part of a mainland during the early origins of mammals but has been separated from the rest of the world for more than fifty million years. During that time, the mammals of Australia proliferated and occupied the available niches in much the same way that mammals did in other places of the world—except that in Australia only pouched-type mammals were available for speciation. Consequently the "wolves," "bears," and "rodents" which originated in Australia were all marsupials (bear their young in pouches) in contrast to the placental mammals of the rest of the world.

The pouched phalangers of Australia are counterparts of the squirrels of north temperate continents. There is even a flying phalanger in Australia, with folds of skin along its sides comparable to the adaptation of its counterpart flying squirrel of America to which it is not closely related. Australian wombats have evolved to a form much like the common woodchuck; bandicoots have long ears and hop like rabbits, but their long tails and noses are more like those of a rat. The Australian koala looks much like a miniature replica of the huge brown bears of the northern continents. There are even blind marsupial "moles" nearly identical in appearance to the common placental moles of North America.

This remarkable resemblance of many marsupial species to placental counterparts clearly indicates that many of the adaptive themes which are successful in given habitats of the world may eventually "come forth," regardless of where or when evolution begins, provided only that the requisite genetic variation is available. In the absence of competing placental mammals, marsupials evolved as "bears," "squirrels," "moles," "rabbits," "cats," "mice," and "wolves." These same themes were accomplished on other continents under similar environmental stresses but stemming from a distinctly different genetic potential.

Species unique in adaptive features also came forth in Australia because the environmental selective pressures as well as the available genetic endowments were also unique. Kangaroos and duck-billed platypuses have no counterparts elsewhere. Also, many species which came forth on continents with climates like Australia's never emerged on that isolated island. Horses, camels, deer, elephants, giraffes, and myriads of other forms never came forth in Australia. Had there been a land-bridge between Australia and other continents, many forms would undoubtedly have immigrated and would have become successful. But, being severely isolated, Australia uniquely evolved those species which could come forth from the genetic variations available on that continent in response to the environmental challenges which were presented. The development of such patchworks of species in response to contrasting environments provides clear evidence that this wonderful display of living organisms is the result of speciation by evolution. Other explanations are essentially implausible.

The continent of Australia, which has about the same area as the United States of America, can obviously support pines, spruces, firs, redwoods, dogs, and rabbits. But before human beings imported them, they had no way of getting there. Since their arrival by humans, many introduced species have spread phenomenally and are even now replacing some of the native species. The "alien" dogs and cats have found Australian marsupials easy prey. Consequently, several native species in Australia now face imminent extinction.

In 1859, twenty-four wild rabbits were delivered to Thomas Austin in Australia. Within three years, they became a pest. Six years later, Austin killed 20,000 rabbits but estimated that 10,000 more were still at large.[1] For over a hundred years they have continued to multiply in Australia. Every conceivable method of controlling their increase has been used; but in this new environment, lacking the predators that have historically kept their population in check, rabbits have had a phenomenal population explosion. Successful speciation is the result of myriads of intricately interacting forces which sculpt out refined balanced communities.

Australian eucalyptus trees, which until a few years ago were found solely in Australia, have become weeds in parts of California where they were introduced. In Australia, eucalyptus trees came forth from the genetic variations available to them there and, in competition with other organisms, filled specific ecological niches to which they were adaptive. Had these same protoplasmic variations been available in California and had the selective forces been present which brought them forth in Australia, California may have also produced eucalyptus trees but perhaps at the expense of, or concomitantly with, other species.

The endemics of a continent or of an island are, therefore, expressions of the available genetic material that can be passed from generation to generation as brought forth by the existing forces of mutation and selection. The genetic combinations necessary for producing placental mammals were just not available in Australia, or they would likely have brought forth some of the same themes that they did in most of the rest of the world, perhaps replacing marsupials.

Apparently marsupials were once widespread throughout the world before placental mammals emerged. Evidence appears both in the fossil record and also by the presence of a few contemporary marsupials as far away from Australia as America. But they have now been replaced almost entirely by placental counterparts.

More primitive than either marsupial or placental mammals are egg-laying mammals (monotremes). Only two living representatives, the spiny anteater and the duck-billed platypus, are still on Earth today, but sixty million years ago they were apparently very successful. Since nearly all egg-laying mammals have become extinct, the added protection for the young furnished by development within the mother's body—as in all placental mammals—has apparently been a very important improvement. Since mammalian eggs usually have very little food stored within them, nourishment is a problem for newly hatched offspring. Marsupial mammals have unique incubators in the form of pouches into which the young crawl soon after birth. In these pouches, the mother's teats provide nourishment for the helpless infant. Obviously this is a great improvement compared to the hazardous route demanded of offspring hatched from eggs.

Care for the young in placental mammals is even more efficient. In these animals, one of the outer membranes of the embryo fuses with the wall of the mother's uterus to form a placenta through which food is transported directly to the developing embryo. The young are thus nourished and protected until they are well developed and ready to be born.

The distribution of marsupials, placentals, and monotremes, isolated and separated from each other in different areas throughout the world, would not likely have been the product of special creation. Had there been only one land mass upon which the animals of the Earth came forth, the sequential replacement of egg-layers by marsupials and subsequently by placentals might by now be complete. Only because of its isolation was Australia able to bring forth its interesting array of primitive marsupials and egg-laying mammals.

The distribution of all plants and animals on the various continents and islands of the Earth declare this same principle. Each family, each genus, each species, appears to have been created from the existing genetic material available within its unique locations in response to local environmental pressures. It is strong evidence that the creation process was not a single event. If each species had come forth as described by creationism, all of the isolated habitats throughout the world would likely have contained the same species.

Because of its severe isolation, New Zealand has also evolved some unique vegetation. Fully three-fourths of all the native species of plants now growing in New Zealand are found nowhere else in the world, although only 10 percent of all plant genera of New Zealand are endemic. Apparently almost all of New Zealand's genera were present before it became isolated as an island; very few of its present-day species were in existence at that time. Nearly all of the various species in New Zealand have come forth since then from the genetic material available within the existing genera. The few endemic genera which must have come forth since the original isolation, testify that isolation was complete a long time ago. It is also interesting to note that most of the non-endemic species of New Zealand are also found in Australia, the nearest neighboring continent. Some New Zealand species are also found in South America, which has caused some students to suggest the presence of an earlier land connection between New Zealand and that continent.

These patterns of distribution offer strong evidence that the Earth has brought forth and is still bringing forth those species of plants and animals that are best qualified for exploiting the particular conditions to which they are exposed. Even though Australia and New Zealand are both isolated islands located in the same part of the world, each brought forth very different plants and animals according to what was best suited for the conditions that existed there. In Australia, more than a hundred unique genera and a thousand species of legumes have come forth. In New Zealand only five genera and only thirteen species of legumes have come forth. Remarkably, seven entire orders of Australian plants are entirely unrepresented in New Zealand. Conversely, New Zealand has no eucalyptus, acacea, or wattles—species that thrive in Australia.

Some islands such as the British Isles, Java, Bermuda, Newfoundland, and Borneo, are known as continental islands because their rock strata indicate that they were, at one time, continuous with a continent. They are usually separated from their neighboring continents by shallow shelves. The plants and animals that live on continental islands often have become isolated populations of the same plants and animals that continued onto the mainland. They lack the striking uniqueness that is found among organisms that live on isolated, non-continental islands. The severity of isolation and the amount of time that has elapsed since the islands separated from the continent are the major factors that influence the degree of divergence of the mainland species and the continental island species.

The plants and animals of England and Scotland have much more in common with those in Europe than with those of Ireland, apparently solely because of the added barrier to migration furnished by the Irish Sea. The absence of snakes in Ireland is much more likely a function of the salt water barrier between the island and the neighboring continent than to the legendary feats of St. Patrick.

Oceanic islands such as the Hawaiian Islands, the Galapagos Islands, and the San Fernandez Islands were never part of continents but were created by volcanic eruptions in the oceans. Their inhabitants show this lack of direct connection by the high rate of endemics. Only those groups which have been able to cross the formidable salt-water barriers are represented. Mammals are conspicuously absent except for bats and seals. Amphibians, snakes, large-seeded dicotyledons, and conifers are all absent because they are so ill adapted for crossing salt-water barriers. Birds, some insects, and weedy plants which can send seed samples by wind or as passengers on birds or floating debris, make up most of the life on oceanic islands.

After arrival on oceanic islands, evolution is often very rapid. The challenge of the new habitats, the wide variations in environments, and the release of old controls provide the machinery for rapid adaptation to new habitats at a phenomenal rate.

Charles Darwin (1809–82) is known as the major originator of the concept of natural selection. During his travels in 1835 to the Galapagos Islands in South America, he collected native finches on these islands that showed a tremendous range in size and in beak characteristics. The thirteen species observed there by Darwin were found nowhere else in the world. In the absence of competition with other genera and species, some finches had adapted to feeding on small seeds, some on large seeds, some on larger fruits, and some on insects. The rapid evolution of different styles of beaks adapted for each type of diet has permitted successful adaptation of many themes. Under severe competition with other bird species on the mainland, finches had a difficult time continuing even as specialists within a single habitat; but with entire new islands at their command, finches rapidly became adapted to many separate niches by different routes.

Other than a few minor exceptions, such as European rats, goats, and pigs introduced by sailors from Europe, all of the animals and plants of the Galapagos Islands have relatives in South America, the nearest continental land mass. But even so, nearly every species of animal and over half of the plants are unique to the islands. Following their chance introduction, they have evolved into unique forms which, in many cases, are different from their ancestors as well as from their cousins in neighboring islands. Some genera of plants found only on the Galapagos Islands are represented by a single unique species on each island. Darwin found, for instance, six species of a tree-like member of the sunflower family, each of which is found only on a single island. All of the islands are near one another, but each is separated by deep water and has arisen separately from volcanic activity. They are thus well insulated one from another. There are not even strong winds to transport insects, birds, or seeds.

These islands, therefore, became a remarkable retreat upon which any chance invader is released from traditional selection pressures and may evolve independently of its relatives, directed only by the influence of its associates or by just plain chance, acting on the available variation. In a limited sense, each island is a new world upon which evolutionary forces may begin anew with any chance immigrant.

It is difficult to explain these peculiar distribution patterns of plants and animals throughout the world on any premise other than that they are the result of the evolutionary process. There is no other plausible way to account for the numerous endemics on isolated islands, for the affinities between species on continental islands and neighboring continents, nor for the convergent and divergent forms of adaptation in similar but isolated habitats. It is both natural and right that the species of the Earth are actually products of the Earth itself, having been brought forth, as planned by God, by a continuation of the very same laws which still affect species today. Alternative explanations such as the special creation of each species, spontaneous generation, or being transported from other planets are entirely inadequate to accommodate the numerous intricate ramifications of this glorious panorama.

Notes

1. P. B. Hamilton, J. R. Stevens, et al., "The Inadvertent Introduction into Australia of *Trypanosoma nabaisi*, the *trypanosome* of the European Rabbit (*Oryctolagus cuniculus*) and Its Potential for Biocontrol," *Molecular Ecology* 14, no. 10 (2005): 3167–75.

7
Embryological Evidence for Evolution

A genetic mutation in the embryos of mice may interfere with the drainage of fluid from the neural canal. This fluid accumulates to form blisters under the skin and interferes with normal development at these points. Mice with this mutation are born with club feet, eye defects, abnormal hair development, and many other monstrous characteristics. All of these aberrations result from just a single minor change in the embryo's DNA.

Mutations that affect an embryo in its early stages of development have a profound effect on subsequent development. Most mutations are harmful, even lethal, and may be discarded as soon as they appear. In humans, some mutations, such as those which affect variations in eye color, hair texture, or the shape of the lips or nose, usually have only a minor impact on the survival or reproductive potential of the organism and often persist and accumulate in populations. But mutations expressed in an embryo during early development affecting the general patterns of development, such as the rate of cell-division, planes of cell division, or the opening or closing of vital ducts may have such a critical impact on survival that they are often lethal and not passed on to subsequent generations. Consequently, most closely related species of plants and animals have very similar embryos and differ mostly in features that develop later. For instance, the ovary of a zucchini squash is almost identical to that of a summer squash; their distinctive differences emerge later. Likewise, early embryos of pigs, cats, and dogs all appear very much alike.

In time, when one species gives rise to others, it involves mainly the accumulation of mutations which occur late in the embryo's development. Over time, as organisms evolve and embryos require more time to mature, many of these features develop earlier and become more protected from the effects of harmful mutations.

Therefore, scientists have come to recognize that each embryo contains evidence of the evolutionary history of the species. Ernst Haeckel (1834–1919), an eminent German biologist, expressed this concept a century ago as the "biogenetic law" which states that "ontogeny recapitulates phylogeny." In other words, an individual organism's biological development, or ontogeny, parallels and summarizes its species' entire evolutionary development, or phylogeny. Although much oversimplified and not completely accurate, this concept can profitably direct our attention to some very interesting phenomena which are incongruous with the concepts of special creation but which are completely harmonious with what would be expected from speciation by organic evolution.

As vertebrate embryos have been studied by biologists, it has become clear that complexity is gradually acquired over long periods of time. Complex organisms are products of the elaboration of simple systems, as may be illustrated by examining embryonic development in three systems: kidneys, cloacae, and hearts.

Embryonic Kidneys

Among living vertebrates, three different kinds of kidneys are sequentially formed during embryonic development for the elimination of waste materials from the body. All vertebrate embryos first develop a simple pronephric kidney, consisting of a series of tubules that draw waste materials directly from the body cavity rather than from the blood. In only a few primitive forms, however, such as the lamprey, does this basic kidney continue to function in mature adults.

In embryos of all higher vertebrates, a second kind of kidney, the mesonephric kidney, develops. This kidney draws waste materials from the blood as it courses through the tissues, draining them off through a tubular duct. This type of kidney continues to be used by mature amphibians and fishes.

Vertebrate embryos subsequently form even a third type of kidney, the metanephric kidney, which differs from its predecessors by being a compact rather than elongated organ. It is this system which continues to be functional in all adult reptiles, birds, and mammals.

As these embryos develop, all three types of kidneys are formed. Most biologists consider their existence to be evidence that vertebrate history included ancestors that probably functioned with pronephric kidneys and, because of greater efficiency, evolutionary descendants that functioned with mesonephric-type kidneys, and later because of greater efficiency, metanephric kidneys.

Embryonic Cloaca

As embryos, humans and all other vertebrates, empty their digestive tract and urogenital canal into a common chamber--the cloaca. Only in placental mammals is a septum formed during later embryonic development that separates these two tracts. Because there are advantages provided by such an innovation, other vertebrates may eventually evolve in that direction provided the requisite genetic mechanisms become available to them.

Embryonic Hearts

Early in the embryonic development of all vertebrates, their hearts undergo a series of distinct changes. At first, the embryonic heart is merely a straight tube—a part of a blood-vessel. This muscularized blood vessel grows at disproportionate rates and assumes an S-shape, consisting of two regions or chambers. Adult fish continue to use this kind of heart which permits the blood to flow through it continuously before going to the gills for oxygenation.

Subsequently, the embryonic heart develops two anterior chambers (auricles) which are separated from each other by a septum which thus permits double circulation of the blood: one circulatory loop to the lungs and the other to the body. This heart is found in amphibians and most reptiles. The embryonic heart continues to undergo further evolution as the lower two chambers (ventricles) also become separated, thus providing the double-circulation system, a structure present in crocodiles, birds and mammals, including human beings. This arrangement allows the blood to be coursed to the lungs (where it is oxygenated) independently of its circulation to the rest of the body.

Adult hearts of all vertebrates, including humans, are derived from simple sequential modifications while developing as embryos. The continuous S-shaped hearts of adult fishes are a relatively minor change from the more primitive straight tubes. The three-chambered hearts of adult reptiles require relatively few adjustments of the embryonic fish-like hearts. The four-chambered hearts of adult mammals are structurally only slightly different from the three-chambered hearts of reptiles. But a direct evolutionary change from a simple muscularized tube to a complex four-chambered heart would have required so many adjustments that it almost certainly could not have suddenly occurred. Four-chambered hearts, as we know them, appear to be structured specifically for correlated activity with lungs and with temperature controlled regulators.

From this premise, biologists have come to recognize that animals which embryonically develop four-chambered hearts share ancestry with animals that embryonically develop only three-chambered hearts. But it does not argue that today's reptiles were the ancestors of modern mammals. In fact, they certainly were not. Modern reptiles and modern mammals may have had common ancestors, but they are both successful contemporary species, simultaneously occupying unique habitats. Neither living group is directly ancestral to the other. Similarly, although we may have had common ancestors, humans did not spring from monkeys because modern humans and modern monkeys both exist and flourish during the same time period and reside in their own unique environmental niches.

The embryonic development of the nervous system, the digestive system, the genital systems, the musculature, and many other structures offer verification that complexity is acquired sequentially. Complex organisms are generally products of the elaboration of simple systems, and embryonic development appears to represent a brief synopsis of embryonic evolutionary history.

Why is the pronephric kidney formed during embryonic growth? Why do gill-slits and vermiform appendices and cloacae appear in an embryo? Most researchers consider the acquisitions of one alteration upon another, accompanied by the elimination of non-functional attributes, and the retention of other vestigial structures not yet discarded as evidence of a lengthy history of organic evolution. Studies of embryonic relationships provide even more evidence that the tissues, structures, species, and phyla of living organisms have indeed been brought forth from the Earth, as declared by the prophets and recorded in the scriptures.

8

Comparative Anatomy as Evidence for Evolution

As biologists study the numerous living organisms on Earth, they have found it helpful to assign each individual plant or animal a formal scientific name that describes the similarities which it shares with other living organisms. One of the first biologists to create such a system was the Swedish scientist Carolus Linnaeus (1707–78). The classification system that he developed, although revised somewhat over the years, has come to be the most widely used taxonomic system into which various life forms are organized. It is based on a simple hierarchical structure: domain, kingdom, phylum, class, order, family, genus, and species. "Kingdom" is a very broad category, and "species" is much more specific. Individuals of the same species share basic genetic similarities and can interbreed and produce fertile offspring.

Because every plant and animal on Earth will eventually die, the only way living organisms can continue to be represented is to leave offspring. All life forms require systems for reproducing and also means for surviving long enough to reproduce. Therefore, the anatomical structures and processes of all plants and animals are involved in some way in promoting greater efficiency in reproduction either directly or by providing advantages for survival.

Because members of the plant kingdom can manufacture their own food by photosynthesis, their success depends almost entirely upon efficiency in reproduction. Such efficiency usually includes modifications of the flowering parts, which ensure high levels of pollination and seed production. Consequently, the principal criteria for distinguishing species and genera and even families of flowering plants are based almost entirely on differences in flower parts.

Since animals cannot manufacture their own food, methods of food procurement have dominated their evolution. All major phyla of animals are distinguished by differences in their digestive tract, and all orders of mammals and insects are distinguished by their food habits. The taxonomy of insects is based on differences in anatomical structures.

These great sweeping themes, which reflect basic similarities and differences in plants and in animals, continue into all levels of biological classification. The members of each family have many characteristics in common. All members of the same genus within a family have, in addition to their family similarities, other characteristics in common; and all species and varieties of the same genus are alike in genus characteristics, family characteristics, class characteristics, and phylum characteristics. The nearest relatives are generally most alike, and from details of similarities, genealogical relationships can often be accurately deduced.

For example the relationships between a Delicious apple and other plant forms can be described in the following heirarchy:

- The plant kingdom is comprised of organisms which have the ability to derive energy through photosynthesis.
- Among the members of the plant kingdom are some which flower and produce seeds enclosed in fruits. These plants, called angiosperms (phylum), are currently the dominant plants on Earth and have been for the past 100 million years.
- There are two orders of angiosperms: monocotyledons and dicotyledons. Those which produce two seed-leaves in the embryonic plants are designated as dicotyledons. Included in this order of plants are violets, buttercups, beans, oaks, and many others.

- The rose family also belongs to the order of dicotyledons. Roses have all the characteristics of angiosperms and dicotyledons but are additionally distinguished by having petals and stamens in multiples of five.
- Apples are members of the rose family that have an inferior ovary and other unique characteristics, in addition to having fruits, two seed-leaves, petals, and stamens in multiples of five.
- And Delicious apples are one variety that shares characteristics with all previous groups and yet has distinctive attributes of its own.

All varieties of apples are more closely related to each other than to varieties of roses, and all roses and apples are more closely related than to other dicotyledenous plants. These similarities suggest that Delicious apples were derived from just one of the many varieties of apples. In fact, Delicious apples actually originated as a mutant seedling at Peru, Iowa, in 1880.

Such genealogical relationships are completely understandable when seen in the context of speciation by organic evolution. However, the tenets of special creation and intelligent design do not require nor do they explain such biological relationships.

The arm of a man, the wing of a bird, and the front leg of a cow superficially may appear to have little in common, but the component bones are embryonically nearly identical. The two front limbs typically consist of a single long bone (humerus), two shorter, parallel bones (radius and ulna), eight wrist bones, five palm bones, and five digits. The hind limbs also have comparable components: one long bone (femur), two parallel leg bones, eight ankle bones, five sole bones, and five digits. Among the vertebrates, some of these bones are greatly reduced in size; some are greatly enlarged. For example, the upper arm bones (humeruses) of bats are rather short, but the radius and finger bones are greatly elongated to become wings. In some animals, certain bones are fused. For example, in hares and rabbits, the lower leg bones are fused for strength in jumping. In other animals such as whales and manatees, the legs are absent altogether, and only a trace of a vestigial pelvis remains where the legs would have been attached. Boa constrictors and pythons also have vestiges of a pelvis and even some hind-limbs, but no other snakes show evidence of remnants of such back limbs. Nevertheless, evidence of the same basic skeletal pattern is found in all four-limbed vertebrates.

Most biologists consider all vertebrates to have come from one common ancestral species. All mammals have seven cervical vertebrae. The tiny mouse, the short-necked elephant, the stiff-necked porpoise, and the long-necked giraffe all have the same number of neck bones! All fishes have a vertebral column, which consists only of a trunk region and a tail region. All amphibians have a trunk region and a tail region, as well as a short cervical and sacral region. Birds, mammals, and some reptiles have a longer cervical area, a trunk divided into a thorax (to which is attached long ribs), and a lumbar region (with very short or no ribs).

All mammals, embryonically, have miniature teeth; but as development proceeds, some embryonic teeth develop into tusks, some into incisors, and some into molars. Although embryonic baleen whales show full potential for a mouth full of teeth, adults haven't a tooth in their head. Cattle have embryonic teeth on both jaws but those on the upper jaw never come through. Why are they even formed? Why do whales and boa constrictors begin to form hind legs which never develop? Why do humans have muscles for fluffing their body hair when cold, even though hair does not develop and all that can be accomplished is the formation of goose-pimples?

There appears to be only one answer. And such a simple, all-encompassing answer it is: "Let the earth bring forth!" From the variations available, by removing the less adaptive individuals, natural selection has sculptured out the more adaptive forms present on Earth.

Vestiges of structures that are no longer functional provide evidence that historically the Earth has brought forth myriads of expressions from the available clay. With continual improvements and adjustments to changing conditions, some attributes and structures which were once essential for survival may be replaced by other systems as they come along. But vestiges of the basic origins from which they were derived may still be evident, particularly in embryonic and infant forms.

The human body possesses many such vestiges of anatomical structures whose previous functions are now mostly lost. We have rudiments of muscles for moving our ears although very few people can get them to work. These same muscles are also rudimentary in anthropoid apes but not in baboons and other primates. We also have muscles similar to those used by other mammals for twitching the skin, but ours are rudimentary and nonfunctional except those with which we wrinkle our foreheads and raise our eyebrows.

Other fascinating features of the human anatomy can also be seen as nonfunctional vestiges of previously functional organs. We have a small nictitating membrane in the corner of each eye which is functionless in the human eye, but is used by birds and some mammals to sweep the eye from the side. A small blunt point in the external fold of the ear is thought to be a relic of pointed ears. Our sinuses have difficulty draining because of the erect way that we carry our heads. Our appendix appears to serve no function at all but can cause problems if it becomes infected. Wisdom teeth appear to be currently disappearing.

Even our sparse body hair seems to be a relic of a previously much more copious growth. Hair patterns among modern primates are particularly suggestive. Only in humans, anthropoid apes, and a few monkeys does the hair on the lower arm point toward the elbow. Some have thought this pattern to be adaptive from a time when our ancestors stood with their hands raised to shoulder height—a posture still common among baboons and chimpanzees today. The downward direction of hair on the back of the hands toward the fingertips is found in all anthropoid apes. Humans, apes, monkeys, and baboons all have sparse hair growth patterns on their fingers: hair is absent on the last segment of the digit, and is often missing on the next to the last segment.

Such anatomical similarities of related organisms provides strong evidence that the nearest relatives of a species differ by simple genetic alternatives and that more distantly related organisms have more extensive genetic differences. If some species had not become extinct, the transitions between species would probably still be evident and the genetic relationships would be clearer. But with the extinction of non-adaptive or less adaptive forms, discontinuities have come to separate most contemporary species. Therefore, it is only because of variation that species have definition .

If our ancestors actually did have well-developed appendices and movable ears, how did these structures erode away to become mere vestiges? Clues to answer such questions have come from experiments dealing with artificial selection. When scientists attempt to select for just one specific trait in an organism, a common result is that there is often a rapid decline in fertility. For instance, a study was undertaken to select for an increased number of bristles on the abdomen of flies (Drosophilia). However, selection was only able to proceed for a few generations before the flies became so infertile and unviable that the lines could not be maintained. Subsequently, when selection was relaxed in such lines, fertility and viability recovered.[1]

Why does this occur? The simplest explanation for this oft-observed feature is that, given intense selection for one or few characteristics, other characteristics may be neglected. Because there are many more ways of being infertile than of being fertile and of being nonviable than viable, when researchers selected for abdominal hairs, there was no focus on selection for viability or fertility. Subsequently the frequency of low fertility and of low viability will quickly increase.

The deterioration of eyesight may be another example of this phenomenon. Considering the many ways of having a nonfunctional eye and the few ways (maybe only one way) of having a perfect eye, unless all alternatives are discarded, the incidence of nonfunctional eyes will quickly increase. This appears to be the cause of the frequent occurrence of blindness in fish and other animals that occupy dark caves. Some fish have eyes greatly reduced in size; some have superficially normal eyes but no functional optic nerve; others have no eyes at all but still have openings in the skull where eyes may have previously existed.

Some biologists consider that human eyes are currently deteriorating for this same reason. Our current standards of selection in many societies place very little disadvantage on persons with defective eyes. Since there are more ways of having defective eyes than perfect ones, degeneration is likely to occur. From the apparent increase of people today who need glasses, contact lenses, or Lasik or other surgeries, it appears that this trend is fairly rapid.

So even though organic evolution provides the means for all living things to constantly acquire new characteristics to increase their adaptability to their environment, much of evolution is simply due to the deterioration of characters which are not favored by natural selection.

Over time, as some characteristics emerge and others disappear, genealogical affinities between species may appear disjunctive; and because of extinction, evidences of relationships may seem difficult to detect. Nevertheless, by comparing anatomical and physiological similarities which exist among all plants and animals, relationships become evident and help bring an understanding of how all life on Earth is connected. Although these biological relationships are not required nor considered vital by those who forward the precepts of intelligent design, they are basic and compatible with the criteria of organic evolution and with the scriptural account, "Let the earth bring forth the living creature after his kind . . . and it was so" (Gen. 1:24)

Notes

1. Graham Bell, *Selection: The Mechanism of Evolution* (New York: Oxford University Press, 2008), 150–53.

9
Biochemical Evidence

All living organisms on Earth are composed of cells, each of which consists of a watery soup contained within a differentially permeable membrane. Through the process of osmosis, water moves through these membranes more readily than other chemicals, resulting in differences in the chemical composition inside and outside of the cells. The watery composition inside the cell allows the cell to be alive; outside is lifeless. This fact has caused most biologists to conclude that life originated in water and that the various species of plants and animals on Earth today represent innovations that permitted them to carry little "oceans of water" confined within these cell membranes to the various habitats of the world.

Plants and animals living in deserts require a good deal of specialized equipment to maintain their aqueous cellular composition. Those living in tide-pools possess a different set of equipment.

A particularly severe challenge attends organisms that live in fresh water. Because of osmosis, cells of these organisms may absorb large quantities of water. Without some way of countering this differential, the cells will swell and burst. Tiny one-celled paramecia have adapted to this challenge by pumping the water back out about as fast as it comes in. Their bodies contain contractile vacuoles in which the incoming water accumulates. When a vacuole is filled, it suddenly contracts and squirts the water out. These little pumps can excrete a volume of water equal to the size of the entire cell every two minutes!

Some organisms living in fresh water have shells or other types of coatings that are sufficiently impervious to water to slow down the rate of absorption. Most plants build a sturdy wall of cellulose around each cell which effectively prevents the cells from swelling and bursting.

Much of the extensive equipment required for survival provides not so much new approaches to life, but rather a means by which basic processes can be carried successfully into new environments.

All forms of life share many basic similarities in their chemical composition. Most species on Earth store energy as ATP (adenosine triphosphate). Every species on Earth synthesizes proteins following a code dictated by RNA (ribonucleic acid). All RNA is built out of a ribose sugar, phosphoric acid, and four nitrogenous bases. The differences between the proteins of any two species of plants and animals is due to differences in the linear arrangement of these four nitrogenous bases. All green plants make chlorophyll of four pyrrol units arranged in a ring around a central atom of magnesium.

A common sugar, glucose, can be manufactured in two forms which differ only in their capacity to rotate polarized light in different directions. One form, D-glucose, rotates light to the right. L-glucose rotates light to the left. Although these two forms of glucose appear to have identical chemical properties, all glucose in all living organisms, both plant and animal, is of the D-form. Similarly, all synthetically created amino acids are of the L-form.

Most scientists interpreted these and many other biochemical similarities shared among all forms of plants and animals as evidence of their common ancestry. It also suggests that life on Earth originated a very long time ago; and since then, many species have emerged to represent a host of unique adaptations. It is difficult to explain these differences in biochemical content by the tenets of special creation, but they are easily accommodated as consequences of natural selection.

Let the Earth bring forth!

Since genes characterize each living species, it is not surprising that gene products provide a direct index of genealogical ties. Specifically ordered amino acids known as polypeptide chains become the building blocks of proteins within living organisms. Some of these polypeptide chains are parts of proteins which contribute to the structure of the bodies of plants and animals. Others become organized into proteins functioning as enzymes. Consequently it might be expected that protein similarities and differences would faithfully reflect ancestral relationships. They do.

In one study, biologists measured the amount of plasma protein found in fish. They found that the proteins generally increased between simple, more primitive fish and more complex fish. Sharks had 2.18 grams of plasma protein, gar 2.87 grams, catfish 2.94 grams, mullets 3.78 grams, and perch 3.70 grams per 100 grams of plasma. Parallel to this increase in total plasma protein is a general increase in complexity of the globulins, a specific type of protein found in blood.[1]

Cytochrome c is a remarkable "tattle-tale" protein that many organisms require for aerobic respiration. It functions in helping to extract energy from foodstuffs. It is a relatively small molecule, consisting of only 104 amino acids. An exciting thing about cytochrome c as an index to genealogy is that the sequence of amino acids is different in the cytochrome c of different organisms. Cytochrome c in humans differs from that in a species of rhesus monkey by only one amino acid. Humans differ from horses in their cytochrome c by twelve amino acids, from pigs by ten and from chickens by fourteen amino acids. There are twenty amino acid differences in cytochrome c between horses and tuna fish, and thirty-one differences between cytochrome c of horses and moths. Yeasts and some of the vertebrates differ by as many as forty-nine amino acids. It is reasonable to conclude that these differences are reflections of genetic mutations accumulated through long series of evolutionary history.

Perhaps even more significant than the differences in cytochrome c is a group of fifty amino acids that are the same in all aerobic organisms. Does this mean that all organisms had common ancestors with the same simple original cytochrome system?

The geographic distribution of various human blood-groups indicates that new types of proteins may accumulate in a relatively short time, perhaps just a thousand years or so. The isolated Basques of northern Spain are almost entirely devoid of Type B blood. The subgroup A2 blood is found mostly in Europe, the Middle East, and Africa. Rh negative blood is very high among the Basques and Africans but is mostly absent among many groups in Asia. It is likewise rare among American Indians and the peoples of the Pacific Islands.

Blood proteins of cattle are so specific that, given a blood sample from any cow, an expert can accurately identify the breed from which the blood was obtained and, in some cases, even the specific herd involved!

In cattle, insulin consists of two long polypeptide chains (A and B) joined together. Sheep, horses, and even whales have exactly the same B chain but differ from each other and from cattle in just three of the amino acids in the A chain.

Therefore, although all forms of life on Earth have many more similarities than differences, each species, each genus, each variety, and each individual is nevertheless somewhat bio-chemically unique. Because these biochemical differences reflect differences in genetic make-up, near relatives are bio-chemically more alike than are more distantly related groups.

As biologists continue to study the biochemical compo-nents of all forms of life, they are able to more accurately determine the genealogical relationships and ancestries of the multitude of plants and animals on Earth. These relationships provide even more evidence of the great plan of God in preparing the Earth to bring forth life through the continuing process of organic evolution.

Notes

1. Gordon Gunter, L. L. Sulya, and B. E. Box, "Some Evolutionary Patterns in Fishes' Blood," *Biological Bulletin*, 121, no. 2 (October 1961): 302–6.

10
Genetic Evidence

Since all expressions of life are derived from genetic information, the best clues to evolutionary history are, ultimately, genetic. Slight differences between individuals of the same population are due to slight genetic differences; larger differences such as those existing between distinct species are due to major genetic differences.

Because a minute change in the structure of a gene may have profound effects on the total organism, it is not difficult to account for the great variety of protoplasmic expressions exhibited by the numerous species of plants and animals on Earth today. For instance, genetic differences account for the differences in color in populations of mice living on white sand and those living on dark clay soils. On dark soils, dark-colored mice are more numerous than light-colored mice because predators have a harder time detecting them. Similarly in areas of white sand, light-colored mice are more numerous than dark-colored mice. These genetic differences provide advantages for survival and, hence, for reproductive potential.

In much the same way, dark-colored peppered moths (*Biston betularia*) increased phenomenally in parts of western Europe during the time that extensive industrialization began in the nineteenth century. Heavy deposits of soot on the bark of trees near centers of industry provided a new camouflage for dark-colored moths but made light-colored moths stand out brightly. Birds that fed on moths were able to detect and therefore consume many more of the light-colored ones. Until the beginning of the industrial revolution, dark-colored moths were a rare collector's item, but subsequently they became increasingly common.[1]

The sequential acquisition of mutations eloquently reflects the evolutionary process but essentially negates interpretations by special creation.

After an initial difference has been established by a simple gene mutation, additional modifications may exaggerate and further isolate such differences until they become irreversible. An excellent illustration of this process appears to have been involved in the evolution of sexuality in different groups of plants and animals. Many plants and most animals have well-defined separate sexes. The absence of separate sexes in many groups, however, and rather weak determiners for sex differentiation in other groups suggest that what is now a profoundly complex attribute of most organisms on Earth may have had rather simple beginnings.

For example, bisexuality in asparagus is determined by a single gene difference. Asparagus plants having genotype *Mm* (or rarely *MM*) are male, and those with the genotype *mm* are female. Nearly all matings are between *Mm* males and *mm* females, resulting in half *Mm* males and half *mm* females in the offspring every generation.

Many species of plants and animals have apparently had a long history with the evolution of bisexuality and have come to exhibit many secondary effects of such separation of sexes. For instance, male deer (bucks) produce antlers; females (does) do not. Male chickens (roosters) are usually larger and develop long tail feathers; females (hens) are smaller and have shorter feathers. The male black widow spider is brown while the female is shiny black with the red hourglass mark on her abdomen. Sometimes male and female characteristics can be seen in the plant kingdom. Female poplar trees produce cotton; male poplars produce catkins.

Most mammals have well-defined sex chromosomes (chromosomes that carry the genes determining sex). Females have two X chromosomes (XX); males have one X and one Y chromosome (XY). Some birds have just the reverse: Males have two Z chromosomes (ZZ), and females have one Z and one W chromosome (ZW).

If XY = male and XX = female, then females do not typically receive the Y chromosome. The Y chromosome is, therefore, a poor place to carry essential genetic information that was valuable for both sexes. The Y chromosome in mammals carries a relatively small number of genes, and none are essential for survival.

Grasshoppers do not have a Y chromosome. Female grasshoppers are XX; male grasshoppers are XO (the "O" means there is no Y chromosome). Vinegar flies (*Drosophila*) are not far behind the grasshoppers. Their Y chromosomes are almost entirely empty; scientists in laboratories can easily produce XO males. Although these males are viable and appear normal, they are sterile. Bisexual species exhibit many degrees of gene paucity in Y chromosomes. Even in humans, the Y chromosome contains relatively few genes.

Interpretations such as these, which have come from extensive research over the past several decades provide compelling evidence in favor of the theory of speciation by organic evolution. Geneticists throughout the world have been able to study the genes and chromosomes in various plants and animals and often reconstruct their ancestral histories. It is extremely difficult to deny the process of evolution as an integral component of the creation process. Special creation does not address the extensive variations expressed in numerous different organisms on Earth, nor does it assess the wealth of genetic information they provide.

Were it not for its rich supply of environmental variations (accommodated by phenotypic plasticity), the Earth could not have brought forth the abundant array of plants and animals that grace our beautiful planet. Were it not for such a rich available supply of genetic variation (accommodated by genetic flexibility), life on this Earth would be extremely dull and monotonous. Furthermore, it would soon become extinct.

Genetic flexibility is the biological process that provides beauty and variety to the face of the Earth. What a marvelous plan God set in motion when He created this Earth in such a way that the constant interplay of plasticity and flexibility could bring forth new species and maintain such an eternally rejuvenating process. "And the Gods said: Let us prepare the earth" (Abr. 4:11).

Notes

1. H. B. D. Kettlewell, "Insect Survival and Selection for Pattern: Most Camouflage and Survival Mechanisms, though Highly Perfected, Can Be Adapted to Changing Environments," *Science* 148. no. 3675 (June 4, 1965): 1290–96.

11
The Quest for Truth

Strangely, some people are wont to separate science and religion as far as possible. But since they are both in a sincere quest of truth, these two groups are at least on parallel, if not convergent, courses.

Faith is the cornerstone of productive religion as well as of productive science. Actually, it may sometimes require more faith to engage in scientific study than in religion.

Scientific quests for truth are restricted to observations about the properties and expressions of matter and phenomena and hence may never completely reveal terminal truths. For instance, a good deal has been learned about gravity. We can measure its effects, calculate its intensity, and prepare counter-forces to negate its effect. But we still do not fully know what it is. We have learned to measure, produce, control, and even dissect light but we still do not fully know what light is. We have discovered properties of chemical bonds, atomic structure, kinetic energy, black holes, neutrinos, heat, sound, and time, but we haven't yet a complete understanding of what they are.

As we learn more about the properties of light, heat, and gravity, our confidence increases about their expected expressions; and this confidence—this faith—is a prerequisite to all scientific pursuits. We have come to expect matter to repeatedly express itself in the same way, under the same conditions, over and over again. We even exercise great faith in incomprehensible phenomena. No one can comprehend time or timelessness, infinite space or infinite randomization. Yet we accept by faith that these are integral processes and attributes of our universe.

In matters of religion, however, a few absolute truths have been given to us from God through inspired prophets. We accept them by faith. God has revealed to us that we are immortal. What a wonderful piece of information this is! Faith in this truth has permitted humankind to rise to transcendent heights. It has permitted us our greatest joy, our greatest hope. If this truth were removed from us, we would be left empty and hopeless. Since we could have never discovered this truth with our own faculties, it alone is sufficient to elicit our love for and worship of Him from whom it came.

God described to us His wondrous plan of salvation and our individual roles in this plan. This also, we could never have discovered on our own. But what a tremendous contribution this revelation has provided! Thousands upon thousands bear witness that faith in this truth has been more significant in their lives than faith in all scientific discoveries combined. It has motivated people toward self-improvement, greater love, deeper compassion, more willing sacrifice, more intense dedication, and more unswerving loyalty. It transcends all human creeds.

Although science and religion have many dissimilarities, because of their common quest for truth they repeatedly converge and, at points of contact, often beautifully suture and coalesce. Both spring from phenomena much too profound to comprehend; but if through faith we accept their validity, our lives are made more meaningful, our goals loftier, and our productivity more vigorous.

Many scientists have gained strong faith in the truthfulness of scientific discoveries, including the role of organic evolution in bringing to pass the creation of life and living organisms. This faith has come from extensive study, from the testimonies of others, and from personal experiences. Some have even had the thrill of synthesizing new species in their laboratories and have discovered the evolutionary process in operation in nature.

We can hope that the truths discovered in our laboratories will become more and more compatible with the truths recorded in the scriptures. God's dictum, "Let the earth bring forth," is a profound declaration about speciation by evolution. The Earth has brought forth and is still bringing forth species after species after species. The concepts of organic evolution, as I understand them, appear to harmonize with the scriptures. Points of disharmony seem few, and these few disparities appear to be the result of either ignorance or misinterpretation. In either case, they will most likely be resolved as new light and knowledge become available.

Some students have been disturbed by the biblical reference to "six days" as the creative period for the Earth. Some have equated a thousand years in human time to a single day with the Lord—which of course would still fail to provide adequate time. Some insist on a literal twenty-four-hour period, which is even less tenable.

Throughout the Bible, the word "day" has been used to denote many different time-periods. In Genesis 2:17, the Lord, while instructing Adam and Eve to refrain from eating the forbidden fruit, warned them, "For in the day thou eatest thereof thou shalt surely die." Although soon after this event, Adam "died" from the presence of God, he lived many more years before dying mortally from the Earth. The day spoken of in Genesis was obviously not the twenty-four-hour period we currently refer to as a day.

In Genesis 2:4 we read, "These are the generations of the heavens and of the earth when they were created, in the day that the Lord God made the earth and the heavens." This day, denoting a summation of the entire creation process, was obviously not the same length of time meant by each of the seven separate "days" described in Genesis 1. Other scriptural passages refer to the "day of temptation" (Heb. 3:8), the "day of trouble" (Ps. 50:15), the "day of his wrath" (Rev. 6:17), the "day of Jerusalem" (Ps. 137:7), the "day of Christ" (Phil. 1:10), the "day of judgment" (Matt. 11:24) and the "day of the Lord" (Joel 2:1). 2 Peter 3:8 states: "One day is with the Lord as a thousand years, and a thousand years as one day." Our finite minds are incapable of comprehending infinite time, infinite distance, infinite matter, or any of the other attributes of eternity. Consequently, when we attempt to circumscribe the creation process into the confines of our limited comprehension, its eternal nature defies our boundaries.

Since the process of creation is still in operation, the days referred to in the Bible must connote a definition of activities rather than events. The initial separation of dry land from the waters, which yielded the continents of the world, was not a sudden event which abruptly stopped after it was completed as proposed by Creationists. The sediments and fossils in exposed rocks testify of a long dynamic history, which is still in process.

Many of our present-day mountains were uplifted from layers of deposits accumulated in extensive seas. Glaciers have several times covered much of northern Europe and North America. The Atlantic and Gulf coasts of the United States are today sinking into the ocean at the rate of about 0.6mm per year.

The entire thin crust of the Earth is in a continual state of flux. The continents and the ocean floors rise, sink, warp, buckle, and shift. Some mountains erode down; others are lifted up. Some lakes disappear with changing climates or with changing geology; others are newly created. Massive glaciers in Greenland are currently melting at an alarming rate; and some scientists estimate that they will have completely disappeared in about a thousand years or less. Throughout the Pacific Ocean, many new islands have sprung up as volcanic mountain tops. If there is anything at all constant about our old planet, it is its inconstancy.

Because the formation of sediments, the eruption of igneous rock, the filling in of lake beds, and the gouging out of new ones is still in process, it is not surprising to find new species of animals and plants still emerging to occupy the new niches. Others face extinction as their habitats disappear. Although plant life originally came into being after the separation of dry land from the waters, as described in Genesis, new species of plants are even now continually being created and others are vanishing. The eternal laws involved in the creation of our planet cannot cease for they are eternal. As new mountains, streams, and islands appear, bringing beauty and variety to the face of the Earth, new permutations of living organisms come forth as new adaptive species and reproduce after their own kind as faithfully as a cast reflects the contour of its mold. Each environmental niche brings forth a corresponding array of matching living species. As new niches arise, new species arise. As former niches disappear, so do their inhabitants.

Within the framework of the beautiful, profound processes of creation, the scriptures indicate a few of the various events which must sequentially follow each other. As I see it, the Earth was expressly created for human beings; but before they could come forth, the waters and the dry land needed to be separated. Seasons, periods of day and night, and an atmosphere needed to be provided. Plants and animals had to be brought forth. Because animals depend on plants for food, the introduction of animals occurred in the "day" after plants became established. And because the beasts of the dry land emerged from the beasts of the oceans, their "day," sequentially, had to begin after marine animals had come forth. These same sequences are evident even today, long after the initial divergence brought forth the first plants, the first fishes, and the first beasts.

Although the scriptures were not prepared as books of science, the clear simple truths expressed therein are compatible with the general outline of evolutionary development. The Bible does not refer explicitly to such basic universal forces as gravity, atomic energy, the laws of relativity, electromagnetic forces, strong and weak nuclear forces, light, or radio-astronomy; but there appear to be few inconsistencies with the panorama depicted by the scriptures and the concepts derived from scientific experiments.

Some individuals have been disturbed by the mutability of species given the statement in Genesis 1 that each plant and animal will reproduce after its "kind." But it is only the restrictions imposed by human interpretations that provide the basis for such apparent discrepancies. It is certainly true that horses reproduce horses, tomatoes reproduce tomatoes, and humans reproduce humans. Life as we know it on Earth is specifically characterized by this pattern of reproduction of each species after its own kind. What a different world it would be if it were otherwise!

Today we smile at Jan Baptist Van Helmont's (1579–1644) formula announced in the sixteenth century for producing mice: "Place some dirty rags together with a few grains of wheat, or a piece of cheese, in a dark place and in a few days they will be transformed into mice." To produce scorpions, "scoop out a hole in a brick, put into it some sweet basil. Lay a second brick upon the first so that the hole will be imperfectly covered. Expose the two bricks to the sun, and at the end of a few days, the scent of the sweet basil, acting as a ferment, will change the herb into a real scorpion."[1] Vapors and emanations were once considered to be the cause of disease. Aristotle taught: "Animals sometimes arise in soil, in plants, or in other animals."[2] Five hundred years ago, Paracelsus described producing humans by placing certain substances in a well-stoppered bottle, burying it in a dung-heap, and pronouncing incantations over it daily. In time, a tiny living human being would appear inside the bottle. He admitted, however, that he had been unable to keep this tiny human alive after removing it from the bottle.[3] Philippo Bonanni (1658–1723) tells of seeing rotten timber produce worms, which turned into butterflies, which in turn became birds and flew away.[4]

That simple scriptural statement has been proven to be true beyond doubt. The herb yields seed and the fruit tree yields fruit "after its kind" (Gen. 1:21). Extensive research has documented conclusively that there is no such thing as "spontaneous generation." The beasts, cattle, and "creeping things" reproduce after their "kind." Every living organism came from a parent of its own kind. However, all tomato seedlings from a parent tomato are not identical. All of Adam's posterity do not look alike. Biological "free agency" provides variations among the offspring of every living creature. Consequently, even though each species reproduces after its kind, there is usually sufficient available genetic variation for a range of expressions within each species. The extensive variation available to domestic chickens has permitted the formation of more than thirty distinctive varieties including the tiny sixteen-ounce bantam and the large thirty-six-ounce cochin.

The variation available to living organisms is the very foundation of their success. It is the only avenue by which improvement is possible. It is the "free agency" of protoplasm. It has provided the opportunity for some beetles to feed on caterpillars, others to feed on snails, and still others on algae. It has provided the opportunity for some humans to live in the arctic regions, others in deserts, and still others in the tropics. It is only because of the genetic variations made available to all forms of life on Earth that our planet has been able to bring forth the herbs, fruit trees, insects, fowls, fish, and other forms of plant and animal life. Were it not for variations that permit continual adjustment to changing conditions, life as we know it could not exist on this planet.

Notes

1. Jan Baptist Van Helmont, quoted in Lois N. Magner, *A History of the Life Sciences*, 2d ed. (New York: Marcel Dekker, 1994).

2. Aristotle, quoted in B. A. Morrey and Charles Bradfield, *The Fundamentals of Bacteriology* (Philadelphia: Cornell University Library, 1917), 264.

3. Walter Pagel, *Paracelsus: An Introduction to Philosophical Medicine in the Era of the Renaissance*, rev. ed. (New York: Karger, 1982), 162.

4. "Buonanni, Filippo," *Complete Dictionary of Scientific Biography* (New York: Charles Scribner's Sons, 2008), http://www.encyclopedia.com. (accessed December 17, 2009).

12
"And the Lord God Formed Man"

"And the Lord God formed man of the dust of the ground" (Gen. 2:7). This single sentence is just about all that has been revealed to us in the scriptures about the creation of the human mortal body. It is, however, quite sufficient. It emphasizes the oft-repeated declaration found throughout the scriptures that God is the author. It also emphasizes the declaration that all life on Earth, ourselves included, stems from the Earth itself. We humans are derived "from dust" and "unto dust" we will return (Gen. 3:19.) The scriptures prophesied that even the "Lord Omnipotent who reigneth, who was, and is from all eternity to all eternity, shall come down from heaven among the children of men, and shall dwell in a tabernacle of clay" (Mosiah 3:5). The elements and processes used in bringing forth grass, birds, and whales are the very same as those used to bring forth human beings.

In this context it is difficult to find arguments against the abundant evidence that the human body came forth from the Earth in much the same manner that all other organisms came forth. Our body is made of the same materials found in other living organisms; we use the same source of energy for growth and metabolism. Our genetic code consists of the same four nitrogenous bases that code the DNA of all living organisms. Biologically, our bodies are not unique.

We are, however, unique in a far more important context, and that is in our special relationship with God. The culminating achievement in the creation of the human body occurred when God "breathed into his [Adam's] nostrils the breath of life and man became a living soul" (Gen. 2:7). Although the emergence of "man" as a biological species may have resulted from a long, gradual evolutionary history, the union of body with spirit results in the souls of humankind.

Apparently, nothing like this had ever happened before on planet Earth. The waters brought forth great whales, the Earth brought forth every herb of the field, and the human body was also formed from the dust of the Earth. But after this body had been brought forth, a spirit-child of God was allowed to occupy it, and it became a living soul!

This dual nature of human beings is declared in the scriptures. We learn, for example: "The spirit and the body are the soul of man" (D&C 88:15); "And fear not them which kill the body, but are not able to kill the soul; but rather fear him which is able to destroy both the soul and body in hell" (Matt. 10:28).

Although spiritual attributes are less easily measured by scientific methods than biological attributes, they are nevertheless abundantly manifest. It is difficult to describe spiritual experiences in words, although nearly everyone is aware of having enjoyed them. Deep feelings of joy, despair, delight, humor, peace, hope, compassion, and love commonly accompany spiritual experiences although even the best of words poorly describe them. Human beings commit deeds of great nobility as well as dastardly heinous acts. Because of our dual nature, we can rise far higher and sink far deeper than any of God's other creations. So even though our spiritual attributes do not lend themselves to scientific analysis, as do biological attributes, they are as real and, of course, much more important.

The concept that the creation of man's body involved a long evolutionary history is completely compatible with everything that has yet been discovered in science. It is also compatible with scripture.

As our human bodies begin to form, much of our embryonic development appears to occur quite separate and independent of our spirit. Most of the early growth of cells, after the union of the sperm and egg, appear and behave the same way as in the early growth stages of all mammals. After the first cell division, we are each a two-celled entity, then four-celled, then eight-celled and so on. Later in development, human embryos begin to differentiate and eventually can be distinguished as human-like fetuses. But during much of our early embryonic growth, our form does not appear to be uniquely human.

This biological fact raises the question: When does the spirit enter a baby's body? Probably no one knows the exact answer to that question. Some consider it to be at the time of conception, others at the moment a baby takes its first breath, and still others at some point between these two. The association of breath with the entrance of the spirit into the body seems to me compatible with the account recorded in 3 Nephi 1:13, when the Savior told Nephi: "This night shall the sign be given, and on the morrow come I into the world." It also appears consistent with the description of Adam's creation in Genesis 2:7: "And the Lord God formed man of the dust of the ground, and breathed into his nostrils the breath of life; and man became a living soul." Logically, the spirit must enter after the time at which cells can separate to form twins or triplets or other multiple births, when more than a single spirit would have been involved.

The miraculous culmination of the birth of a human being is the result of a series of developmental changes, each of which is required for all subsequent stages. Faulty placenta, incompatible blood groups, contact with recreational drugs, and other stresses eliminate many bodies before they become fully formed. A living soul is a priceless creation! According to Moses 1:39, it was for us that the world was created: "For behold, this is my work and my glory—to bring to pass the immortality and eternal life of man."

Numerous such evidences consistently point to an interpretation of scriptural accounts that the human body was prepared from the dust of the Earth, and it appears that these same processes were also used to bring forth all of God's other creations. The creation process is succinctly expressed in

Abraham 4:11: "And the Gods said: Let us prepare the earth to bring forth." The laws established in the beginning, were evidently formulated for this very purpose. The Earth was prepared to bring forth. It has been and still is magnificently fulfilling that destiny.

"And the Gods formed man from the dust of the ground, and took his spirit (that is, the man's spirit), and put it into him; and breathed into his nostrils the breath of life, and man became a living soul" (Abr. 5:7). Although Adam became "a living soul," he was apparently preceded by many other forms of life including dinosaurs, birds, insects, and mammals. There is also evidence that Adam was preceded by various human-like species.

Adam's body, brought forth from the dust of the ground, was created in the express image of God: "And God said, Let us make man in our image, after our likeness. So God created man in his own image, in the image of God created he him" (Gen. 1:26–27). Adam and Eve's biological ancestors and their associates were magnificent biological creations, evidence of God's wondrous plan in creating the earth to bring forth physical bodies to house His spirit children.

If indeed the human body came forth from the dust of the ground, as the scriptures describe for the creation of other organisms, then could Adam have possibly associated with other biologically similar human-like forms of life? Indeed, Genesis suggests this possibility:

> And it came to pass, when man began to multiply on the face of the earth, and daughters were born unto them,
>
> That the sons of God saw the daughters of men that they were fair; and they took them wives of all which they chose. . . .
>
> There were giants in the earth in those days; and also after that when the sons of God came in unto the daughters of men, and they bare children to them, the same became mighty men which were of old, men of renown. (Gen. 6:1–2, 4)

This passage does not verify that other beings besides the children of Adam and Eve lived with them; but since it specifically notes that there were "giants in the earth in those days" and that "the sons of God came in unto the daughters of men," it suggests that, alternatively, the sons of God may have also "come in unto" others besides the daughters of men.

Adam and Eve had numerous descendants. In the ensuing years, their descendants have spread throughout the Earth and hold within their power the capacity to destroy it.

Whether Adam and Eve's bodies were created from the dust of the ground by God's immediate and personal intervention as proposed by creationists or whether that bodily creation resulted from forces of natural selection over a long period of time as taught by biologists is probably not the crucial question. In either case, God was the author, the omnipotent Creator. All evidences, both theological and scientific, suggest that the same laws that were established in the beginning have been responsible for all of the physical and biological expressions that we still witness today. They appear to include the very same eternal laws that govern all of God's creations. How entirely appropriate that they would have interacted to also create the physical bodies of human beings.

13
Evolution and the Scriptures

"In the beginning God created the heaven and the earth" (Gen. 1:1).

The transcendant message of all scripture is contained in that powerful opening statement. God is the Creator both of heaven and of earth.

The Bible was not written as a book of science, and it is not surprising to find that it contains very little reference to the physical laws of the Earth. Less is mentioned about astronomy, chemistry, mathematics, and biology than about the eternal principles of faith, hope charity, joy, compassion, and repentance. Endowed with God-given faculties which permit experimentation, documentation, and measurement, we are capable of discovering some of the physical laws governing the Earth and it is quite clear that God intended that we should do so: "Thus I, Abraham, talked with the Lord, face to face, as one man talketh with another; and he told me of the works which his hands had made" (Abr. 3:11). The Prophet Joseph Smith taught, "One of the grand fundamental principles of 'Mormonism' is to receive truth, let it come from whence it may!"[1] The great eternal truths given through the prophets by revelation are for the edification of all who will listen: "Do unto others," "judge not," "though your sins be as scarlet . . . ," " . . . a contrite spirit . . . ," "blessed are the meek." These truths give direction, hope, and meaning far beyond anything which can emanate from our laboratories.

During the past century, scientists have discovered a great deal about the Earth and the universe—more than had been known in all the rest of human history. These scientific discoveries are harmonious with the truths found in the scriptures. This congruence is not at all surprising. There can be no conflict in truth. Truths revealed to us through the prophets can in no wise be incompatible with truths revealed to us in our laboratories. Apparent inconsistencies disappear as we gain more understanding. This dynamic process is particularly true relative to the origin of species on Earth.

"Let the earth bring forth," is God's royal command (Gen. 1:11). God prepared an earth that *would* bring forth. All that was required was to let the Earth fulfill its destiny. As it did so, God was pleased with the outcome:

> And God said, 'Let the waters bring forth abundantly, the moving creature that hath life and fowl that may fly above the earth in the open firmament of heaven.
> And God created great whales and every living creature that moveth, which the waters brought forth abundantly, after their kind, and every winged fowl after his kind: and God saw that it was good. . . .
> And God made the beast of the earth after his kind, and cattle after their kind, and every thing that creepeth upon the earth after his kind: and God saw that it was good. . . .
> And God saw every thing that he had made, and, behold, it was very good. (Gen. 1:20–21, 25, 31)

God prepared an earth with an amazing variety of environments. He prepared mountains, streams, meadows, deserts, swamps, shorelines, and oceans arranged on a revolving sphere that moved rhythmically between light and dark, receiving warmth from the sun, and climates ranging from the arctic to the tropical and every gradation in between. The Earth was prepared to bring forth an atmosphere with appropriate gases and rocks with appropriate minerals. "And the Gods said: Let us prepare the earth to bring forth grass; the herb yielding seed; the fruit tree yielding fruit, after his kind, whose seed in itself yieldeth its own likeness upon the earth; and it was so, even as they ordered" (Abr. 4:11).

Being properly prepared, there could be no alternative to these processes. Operating within the framework of these conditions, with these laws, the Earth *would* bring forth. The numerous intricacies involved in the creation process were not the product of chance. God established them as the most probable and the most predictable of all alternatives.

The scriptures tell us that God created whales, grass, and birds, but it does not describe a species-by-species creation, nor is there any indication that species were transferred from other worlds. The account is straightforward and beautiful: "Let the earth bring forth. . . . Let the waters bring forth." God prepared an earth which would do just that. The Earth has brought forth plants and animals which reproduce after their own kind as demonstrated by organic evolution.

Through God's gracious endowments, we human beings have been permitted to glimpse the processes by which the Earth has been, and still is, bringing forth. These processes allow each species to come forth and reproduce its own kind. We have even been able to deliberately create a few new species using these same laws established by God. We have also caused the extinction of several species and have greatly modified others. All of this activity occurs within the framework of the eternal laws established by God from the beginning which provided that the Earth would bring forth.

What a beautiful panorama is presented by the Earth, sculpted into myriads of mountains, valleys, rivers, small streams, dry deserts, and steaming tropics, clothed with a corresponding variety of plants and animals, each adapted to its own environment, each reproducing after its own kind, each preserving its identity, and yet through genetic variations each yielding new adapted descendants. The story was revealed to us in the holy scriptures, but only now, through the union of scientific truths discovered in our laboratories and the truths described in the scriptures, has the account been made so fully comprehensible. Not only is the concept of organic evolution compatible with the gospel as found in the scriptures, it is the very heart of it!

Let the Earth bring forth and let each species so brought forth reproduce after its own kind. It has taken us many years of experimentation and meditation to understand those beautiful, concise statements found in the scriptures. It still requires an effort from most of us to express them. But they encapsulate all that we have learned about the creation process.

The Earth has brought forth permutations of protoplasm adaptive to the environmental niches available to it. For these adaptive units to succeed and to continue, they must reproduce after their own kind. Not only is this the principal message related in Genesis about the creation process, but it is also the principal message elucidated by Darwin. It is unfortunate that so many have interpreted Charles Darwin's contributions as conflicting with the teachings of the scriptures when in reality they furnish strong supporting testimony.

The message in the Bible is clear and concise: The Earth brought forth life as God prepared it to do. Out of the dust of the ground were created all plants, animals, and human beings. As each generation passes away, new ones arise. As each organism returns to the dust, those same elements may then become part of a beetle, a bird, or a fig tree. On and on into eternity, as long as the Earth exists, eternal biological progression—organic evolution—will continue to bring forth from the Earth other well-adapted species. "O how great the plan of our God!" (2 Ne. 9:13)

Notes

1. Joseph Smith Jr. et al., *History of the Church of Jesus Christ of Latter-day Saints*, edited by B. H. Roberts, 2d ed. rev. (6 vols., 1902–12, Vol. 7, 1932; rpt., Salt Lake City: Deseret Book, 1978 printing): 5:498.

Subject Index

acacea, 37
Achard, Franz Karl, 13
Adam and Eve, x, xi, 68, 72–75
adaptation, evidence of, 51
adaptability. *See* genetic flexibility.
Africa, 31, 58
alfalfa, 20
algae, 69
allopolyploids, 21–24
American Indians, 58
amino acids, 57–58
amphibians, 37, 43, 44, 50
angiosperms, 48–49
animals, reproduction of, 48
anteaters, 32, 35
anthropoid apes, 51
appendix. *See* veriform appendix.
apples, 32, 48–49
araucarias, 28
Aristotle, 68
Asia, 32, 58
asparagus, 60
Atlantic Ocean, 66
atomic energy, 67
ATP (adenosine triphosphate), 56
Austin, Thomas, 34
Australia, 13, 31–37
autopolyploids, 20–21

baboons, 32, 51
Bacon, Francis, vii, viii
baleen whales. *See* whales.
bananas, 31–32
bandicoots, 33
Basques, 58
bats, 31, 37
beans, 32, 48
bears, 32, 33
beetles, 69, 80
beets, 13
Bergh, Berthold O., xvi
Bermuda, 37
beryllium, 27
Bible. *See* science and religion.
Big Bang, xvii
biochemistry, and evolution, 55–58
birds, 27, 28, 37, 38, 43, 44, 49, 50, 51, 59, 61, 68, 71, 74, 79, 80
bisexuality, 60
bitterbrush, 15–16
black holes, 63
black widow spiders, 60
blindness, 13, 52
blood types, 60
boa constrictors, 32, 50
Bonanni, Philippo, 68

bones, 49–50
Borneo, 37
British Isles, 37
buttercups, 48
butterflies, 68

cabbage, 23
California, 31, 34
camels, 33
carrots, 3, 5
caterpillars, 69
catfish, 57
Catholic Church, viii
cats, 31, 33–34
cattle, 17, 50, 58, 60, 68, 70
Central America, 32
chard, 13
chemical bonds, 63
chickens, 57, 60, 69
Chile, 16
chimpanzees, 32, 51
chlorophyll, 56
chromatids, 19
chromosomes, 19–20, 22–23,
    60–61. *See also* DNA.
cinnamon, 28
class (taxonomic), 47
cliffrose, 15–16
cloaca, embryonic, 43
club mosses, 27, 29
coal beds, 27, 29
cocoa, 32
coffee, 32
colchicine, 22–23
comparative anatomy, 47–53
competition. *See* environment.
conifers, 28, 37
continental islands, 37
Copernicus, Nicholas, xx
Corbett, William, 16–17
corn, 3, 12, 32

cotton, 21–23
cows. *See* cattle.
creation, process of, xvii–xviii,
    67–68, 78–79. *See also*
    science/religion.
creationism
    and hybridization, 17
    and geology, 66
    and mutations, 60
    arguments against, 7–8, 36,
        39, 42, 56, 61
    beliefs of, xix, 49
crocodiles, 29, 44
crust, of earth, 66
cucumbers, 31
cycads, 28
cytochrome c, 57

Darwin, Charles, vii–x, xxi, 38, 80
"day," possible meanings, 65–66
DDT, 10–11
deer, 33, 60
Delicious apples, 48
dicotyledons, 37, 48
dinosaurs, 2, 28–29
disease, 68
distribution patterns, 31–39
DNA, 19, 71
dogs, 31, 34, 62
duck-billed platypus, 33, 35

ears, 51
Earth. *See* creation.
earthworms, 3
eggplants, 32
electromagnetic forces, 67
elephants, 31, 33, 50
elk, 32
elms, 32
embryos, 41–45, 72–73
endemic species, 31–34, 36

England, 37
environment, as "opposition," 2, 3–4, 36, 38
enzymes, 57
eucalyptus trees, 31, 34, 37
Europe, 32, 37, 58, 66
Evenson, William E., x
evolution, evidence for, xviii, xxii, 25–62, 65–69
extinction, 9, 27, 34, 52, 67, 79
eyes, 51, 52, 53

Fairbanks, Dan, xvi
faith. See science/religion.
family (taxonomic), 47
ferns, 27–29
fertility. See reproduction.
figs, 28, 80
finches, 38
fingers, 51
firs, 32, 34
First Presidency, on evolution, x–xi, xiii
fish, 13, 43, 44, 50, 52, 57, 69
flies, 52
flowering plants, 27–28
fossils, 2, 25–30
fowls, 69
France, 16
free agency, biological, 7, 14, 68
frogs, 31
fruit flies, 10
fruit trees, 3
fundamentalists, rise of, ix
"Fundamentals, The," ix

Galapagos Islands, 37–39
Galileo, vii–viii
gar, 57
genes, 11–12, 57
genetic flexibility, 5–8, 59–62, 69

genetic histories, 61
genital systems, 45
genotypes, 60
genus (taxonomic), 47
gill-slits, 45
ginkgo trees, 28–29
giraffes, 31, 32, 33, 50
glaciers, 66
glucose, 56
goats, 38
gorillas, 32
grass, 17, 20, 23, 71, 79
grasshoppers, 61
gravity, 63, 67
Greenland, 28, 66
Gulf coast, 66
gymnosperms, 27

Haeckel, Ernst, 42
hair patterns, 51
hares, 49, 53
harmony, science/religion. See science/religion.
Hawaiian Islands, 37
hawthorns, 12
hazelnuts, 32
hearts, embryonic, 43–45
heat, 63
heliocentric solar system, ix, xix–xxi
herbs, 72
heterosis, 20. See also hybrids.
hippopotami, 31
horse-tail ferns, 27, 29
horses, 13, 29, 31, 33, 57, 58, 68
human beings, 49, 52, 57, 71–75
Huxley, Thomas Henry, ix
hybrids, 15, 16–17, 22–23

ice age, 2
ichthyosaurs, 29

Inchofer (priest), xx
India, 17, 32
infertility. *See* reproduction.
insects, 27, 69
intelligent design, x, 49, 53. *See also* creationism.
Ireland, 37
Irish Sea, 37
isolation, 9, 15, 31–39

Java, 37
Jeffery, Duane E., x, xv
junipers, 31

kangaroos, 31
kidneys, embryonic, 42–43
kinetic energy, 63
kingdom (taxonomic), 47
koalas, 31, 33

Lake Bonneville, 20–21
lamprey, 43
Landeen, Ellen, xvi
larches, 32
legumes, 36–37
leopards, 32
light, 63, 68
limbs, in embryo, 49
Linnaeus, Carolus, 47
lions, 32
lizards, 3, 13
llamas, 32
Luther, Martin, viii, xx

magnesium, 56
magnolias, 28
mammals, 28, 29, 31–37, 43–44, 48, 50–51, 60–61
manatees, 49
mangels, 13
marsupial moles, 13, 33

marsupial rats, 31
marsupials, 32–36
Mediterranean Sea, 30
meiosis, 19, 22
Meldrum, D. Jeffrey, xi
Mesocordilleran geosyncline, 28
mesonephric kidney, 43
metanephric kidney, 43
meteorites, age of, 27
mice, 6, 12–13, 33, 41, 59, 68
Middle East, 58
mitosis, 19
moles, 33
monkeys, 45, 51
monocotyledons, 48
monotremes, 35–36
moose, 32
Mormonism and Evolution: The Authoritative LDS Statements, x
mosquitoes, 10–11
moths, 57, 59, 60
Mount Ararat, xii
mullets, 57
mutability of species, 67
mutations, 9–14, 23–24, 41–42, 49, 60

natural selection, xxi. *See also* evolution.
nervous system, 45
neutrinos, 63
New Zealand, 31–32, 36–37
Newfoundland, 37
Newton, Isaac, ix
Niessen, Richard, xiii
North America, 31–33, 66
nuclear forces, 67

oaks, 32, 48
oceanic islands, 37–39
On the Origin of Species, x, vii, viii, xx

opossums, 29, 31
order (taxonomic), 47
organic evolution. *See* evolution.
osmosis, 55
ostriches, 32
other planets, lifeforms transported from, 28, 39

Pacific Islands, 58
Pacific Ocean, 66
Pack, Frederick J., xi
palms, 28
paramecia, 55–56
Paracelsus, 68
penicillin, 11
peppers, 32
perch, 57
Peru, Iowa, 49
phalangers, 32–33
phenotypic plasticity, 2–4, 61–62, 69
phylum (taxonomic), 47, 48
pigs, 38, 57
pines, 28, 31, 32, 34
placental mammals. *See* mammals.
plants, reproduction of, 47–48
pleiosaurs, 29
polar bears, 31
polypeptide chains, 57–58
polyploidy, speciation by, 9–10, 19–24
porpoise, 50
potassium, 27
potatoes, 20, 32
pre-Adamites, xi, 74–75
primates, 51
pronephric kidney, 42–43, 45
proteins, 57
public education, and evolution, x
pythons, 50

quantum speciation, 22

rabbits, 6, 32–34, 49
radio-astronomy, 67
radiocarbon dating, 26
radishes, 5, 23
raspberries, 20, 32
rats, 33, 38
redwoods, 28, 31, 34
relativity, 67
reproduction, 47–48, 51–52, 67–68
reptiles, 43–45, 51
rhesus monkeys, 57
rhinoceroses, 32
RNA (ribonucleic acid), 56
rodents, 32
rose, 49
rutabaga, 21, 23
rye, 10, 22

sagebrush, 31
Sager, Carrie, x
salamanders, 3, 13
Salisbury, Frank B., xi
salt deposits, 30
saltbush, 21
San Fernandez Islands, 37
science/religion, harmony of, viii–x, xv, xix, 63–69, 77–80
scorpions, 68
Scotland, 37
scriptures. *See* science/religion.
seals, 37
sedimentary rocks, 30, 66
sequoias. *See* redwoods.
sexuality, 9–10, 15–18, 60–62
shadscale, 20–21
sharks, 57
sheep, 16, 58

sinuses, 51

sloths, 32

Smith, Joseph, 77

snails, 69

snakes, 31, 37

snapdragons, 13

sorghum, 32

soul/spirit, 72–75. *See also* human beings.

sound, 63

South America, 31–32, 38

special creation. *See* creationism.

speciation, 6–7, 9, 23, 47, 66–67

species (taxonomic), 47

spiny anteater, 35

spontaneous generation, 39, 68

spruces, 32, 34

squirrels, 32–33

St. Lawrence Valley, 12

Stebbins, G. L., xv

Stephens, Trent D., xi

sterility, 21–22, 61

Stokes, William Lee, xi

strawberries, 16–17

Stutz, Howard C., xi–xii

Stutz, Mildred, xvi

sugarbeets, 13

sugarcane, 17

sunflowers, 38

survival, advantages in, 47, 60–61

Talmage, James E., xi

taxonomic systems, 47

teeth, 50–51

Texas, 17

tigers, 32

time, 63–64

tomatoes, 31–32, 68

trilobites, 2

Triticale, 22–23

truth. *See* science/religion.

tuatara, 31

tuna fish, 57

turnips, 23

"two books" doctrine, vii, xi, xii

uranium, 27

Utah, salt deposits in, 30

Utah State University, 23

Van Helmont, Jan Baptist, 68

Vatican Observatory, viii

vermiform appendix, 45

vinegar flies, 61

violets, 48

Voices for Evolution, x

volcanoes, 37–38, 66

Waddington, Conrad H., 8

walnuts, 28, 32

water, 55–56

watermelon, 32

wattles, 37

weasels, 32

western United States, xii, 15–16, 20, 28

Westminster Abbey, ix

whales, 49, 50, 58, 71, 72, 79

wheat, 21–23

Wilberforce, Samuel, ix

willows, 32

wolves, 32–33

wombats, 31, 33

woodchuck, 33

worms, 68

yaks, 32

yeasts, 57

Young Earth Creationists, x, xi, xiii. *See also* creationism.

zebras, 32

Scripture Index

Bible

Genesis 1:1 - xvii, 8, 77
Genesis 1:11 - 7, 9, 78
Genesis 1:12 - 21
Genesis 1:20 - xxii, 78
Genesis 1:21 - xxi, 68, 78
Genesis 1:24 - xxi, xxii, 53
Genesis 1:25 - 78
Genesis 1:26–27 - 74
Genesis 2:4 - 65
Genesis 2:7 - 71, 72, 73
Genesis 2:17 - 65
Genesis 2:19 - xxi–xxii, 12
Genesis 3:19 - 71
Genesis 6:1–2 - 74
Genesis 6:4 - 74
Joshua 10:12–13 - xx
Job 12:8 - vii
Psalms 50:15 - 65
Psalms 137:7 - 65
Joel 2:1 - 65
Matthew 10:28 - 72
Matthew 11:24 - 65

Philippians 1:10 - 65
Hebrews 3:8 - 65
2 Peter 3:8 - 65
Revelation 6:17 - 65

Book of Mormon

2 Nephi 2:11–12 - 1
2 Nephi 9:13 - 80
Mosiah 3:5 - 71
3 Nephi 1:13 - 73
3 Nephi 9:15 - xvii
3 Nephi 9:18 - xvii

Doctrine and Covenants

88:15 - 72
93:36 - xix

Pearl of Great Price

Moses 1:39 - xviii, 73
Abraham 3:11 - 77
Abraham 4:11–12 - xviii, 8, 9,
    14, 62, 74, 79
Abraham 5:7 - 74

About the Author

Howard C. Stutz, emeritus professor of genetics at Brigham Young
University, devoted more than sixty
years to the study of genetics and
plant evolution. Born in Cardston,
Alberta, Canada, in 1918, he received
his B.S. (1940) from Brigham Young
University, where he was also awarded
his M.S. in botany (1954), followed by
his Ph.D. in genetics at the University
of California, Berkeley (1956). He
taught at Brigham Young University for
more than thirty years where he received the Karl G. Maeser
Award for Teaching Excellence. Other honors include a
Guggenheim fellowship for his work in the Middle East, a
National Science Foundation grant for his studies in Morocco and
Spain, and a Fulbright fellowship for research and teaching at the
American University of Beirut. He published more than eighty scientific papers.

Dr. Stutz served diligently in many Church callings, including
as a bishop, high councilor, and stake patriarch. He passed away in
2010 shortly after finishing the manuscript for this book. *Let the
Earth Bring Forth* grows out of his love for the Lord and the won-
der and fascination which he exhibits for this magnificent planet
created by God.

Also available from
GREG KOFFORD BOOKS

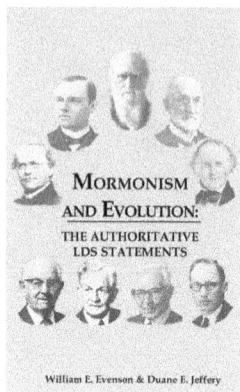

Mormonism and Evolution: The Authoritative LDS Statement

Edited by William E. Evenson and Duane E. Jeffrey

Paperback, ISBN: 978-1-58958-093-0

The Church of Jesus Christ of Latter-day Saints (the Mormon Church) has generally been viewed by the public as anti-evolutionary in its doctrine and teachings. But official statements on the subject by the Church's highest governing quorum and/or president have been considerably more open and diverse than is popularly believed.

This book compiles in full all known authoritative statements (either authored or formally approved for publication) by the Church's highest leaders on the topics of evolution and the origin of human beings. The editors provide historical context for these statements that allows the reader to see what stimulated the issuing of each particular document and how they stand in relation to one another.

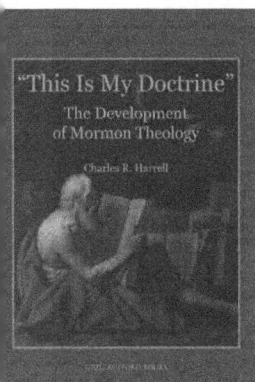

"This is My Doctrine": The Development of Mormon Theology

Charles R. Harrell

Hardcover, ISBN: 978-1-58958-103-6

The principal doctrines defining Mormonism today often bear little resemblance to those it started out with in the early 1830s. This book shows that these doctrines did not originate in a vacuum but were rather prompted and informed by the religious culture from which Mormonism arose. Early Mormons, like their early Christian and even earlier Israelite predecessors, brought with them their own varied culturally conditioned theological presuppositions (a process of convergence) and only later acquired a more distinctive theological outlook (a process of differentiation).

In this first-of-its-kind comprehensive treatment of the development of Mormon theology, Charles Harrell traces the history of Latter-day Saint doctrines from the times of the Old Testament to the present. He describes how Mormonism has carried on the tradition of the biblical authors, early Christians, and later Protestants in reinterpreting scripture to accommodate new theological ideas while attempting to uphold the integrity and authority of the scriptures. In the process, he probes three questions: How did Mormon doctrines develop? What are the scriptural underpinnings of these doctrines? And what do critical scholars make of these same scriptures? In this enlightening study, Harrell systematically peels back the doctrinal accretions of time to provide a fresh new look at Mormon theology.

"This Is My Doctrine" will provide those already versed in Mormonism's theological tradition with a new and richer perspective of Mormon theology. Those unacquainted with Mormonism will gain an appreciation for how Mormon theology fits into the larger Jewish and Christian theological traditions.

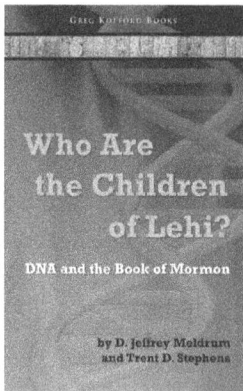

Who Are the Children of Lehi? DNA and the Book of Mormon

D. Jeffrey Meldrum and Trent D. Stephens

Hardcover, ISBN: 978-1-58958-048-0
Paperback, ISBN: 978-1-58958-129-6

How does the Book of Mormon, keystone of the LDS faith, stand up to dat about DNA sequencing that puts the ancestors of modern Native American in northeast Asia instead of Palestine?

In *Who Are the Children of Lehi?* Meldrum and Stephens examine th merits and the fallacies of DNA-based interpretations that challenge the Boo of Mormon's historicity. They provide clear guides to the science, summariz the studies, illuminate technical points with easy-to-grasp examples, and spe out the data's implications.

The results? There is no straight-line conclusion between DNA evidenc and "Lamanites." The Book of Mormon's validity lies beyond the purview c scientific empiricism—as it always has. And finally, inspiringly, they affirr Lehi's kinship as one of covenant, not genes.

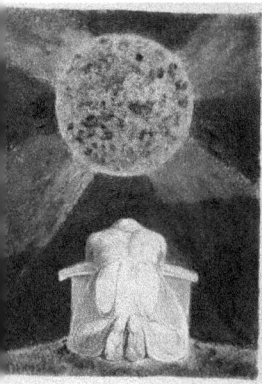

Perspectives on Mormon Theology Series

Brian D. Birch and Loyd Ericson, series editors

(forthcoming)

This series will feature multiple volumes published on particular theological topics of interest in Latter-day Saint thought. Volumes will be co-edited by leading scholars and graduate students whose interests and knowledge will ensure that the essays in each volume represent quality scholarship and acknowledge the diversity of thought found and expressed in Mormon theological studies. Topics for the first few volumes include: revelation, apostasy, atonement, scripture, and grace.

The *Perspectives on Mormon Theology* series will bring together the best of new and previously published essays on various theological subjects. Each volume will be both a valued resource for academics in Mormon Studies and an illuminating introduction to the broad and sophisticated approaches to Mormon theology.

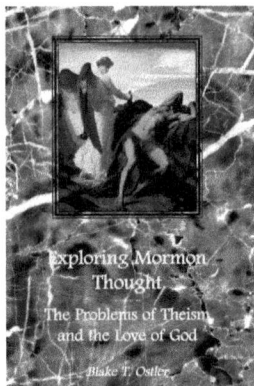

Exploring Mormon Thought Series

Blake T. Ostler

In volume one, *The Attributes of God*, Blake T. Ostler explores Christia and Mormon notions about God. ISBN: 978-1-58958-003-9

In volume two, *The Problems of Theism and the Love of God*, Blake Ostl explores issues related to soteriology, or the theory of salvation. ISBN: 978-: 58958-095-4

In volume three, *Of God and Gods*, Ostler analyzes and responds the arguments of contemporary international theologians, reconstructs an interprets Joseph Smith's important King Follett Discourse and Sermon in tł Grove, and argues persuasively for the Mormon doctrine of "robust deificatior ISBN: 978-1-58958-107-4

Praise for the *Exploring Mormon Thought* series:

"These books are the most important works on Mormon theology ev written. There is nothing currently available that is even close to the rigor ar sophistication of these volumes. B. H. Roberts and John A. Widtsoe may ha had interesting insights in the early part of the twentieth century, but the had neither the temperament nor the training to give a rigorous defense their views in dialogue with a wider stream of Christian theology. Sterlir McMurrin and Truman Madsen had the capacity to engage Mormon theolog at this level, but neither one did."

—Neal A. Maxwell Institute, Brigham Young University

Discourses in Mormon Theology: Philosophical and Theological Possibilities

Edited by
James M. McLachlan and Loyd Ericson

Hardcover, ISBN: 978-1-58958-103-6

A mere two hundred years old, Mormonism is still in its infancy compared to other theological disciplines (Judaism, Catholicism, Buddhism, etc.). This volume will introduce its reader to the rich blend of theological viewpoints that exist within Mormonism. The essays break new ground in Mormon studies by exploring the vast expanse of philosophical territory left largely untouched by traditional approaches to Mormon theology. It presents philosophical and theological essays by many of the finest minds associated with Mormonism in an organized and easy-to-understand manner and provides the reader with a window into the fascinating diversity amongst Mormon philosophers. Open-minded students of pure religion will appreciate this volume's thoughtful inquiries.

These essays were delivered at the first conference of the Society for Mormon Philosophy and Theology. Authors include Grant Underwood, Blake T. Ostler, Dennis Potter, Margaret Merrill Toscano, James E. Faulconer, and Robert L. Millet

Praise for *Discourses in Mormon Theology*:

"In short, *Discourses in Mormon Theology* is an excellent compilation of essays that are sure to feed both the mind and soul. It reminds all of us that beyond the white shirts and ties there exists a universe of theological and moral sensitivity that cries out for study and acclamation."

-Jeff Needle, Association for Mormon Letters

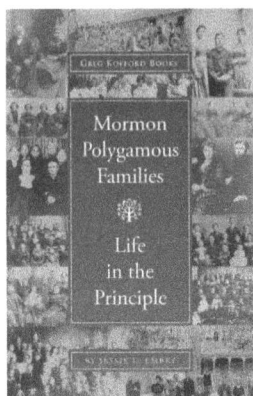

Mormon Polygamous Families:
Life in the Principle

Jessie L. Embry

Paperback, ISBN: 978-1-58958-098-5

Mormons and non-Mormons all have their views about how polygamy wa practiced in the Church of Jesus Christ of Latter-day Saints during the la nineteenth and early twentieth centuries. Embry has examined the participan themselves in order to understand how men and women living a nineteent century Victorian lifestyle adapted to polygamy. Based on records and or histories with husbands, wives, and children who lived in Mormon polygamo households, this study explores the diverse experiences of individual families ar stereotypes about polygamy. The interviews are in some cases the only sourc of primary information on how plural families were organized. In additio children from monogamous families who grew up during the same period we interviewed to form a comparison group. When carefully examined, most the stereotypes about polygamous marriages do not hold true. In this wo it becomes clear that Mormon polygamous families were not much differe from Mormon monogamous families and non-Mormon families of the sam era. Embry offers a new perspective on the Mormon practice of polygamy th enables readers to gain better understanding of Mormonism historically.

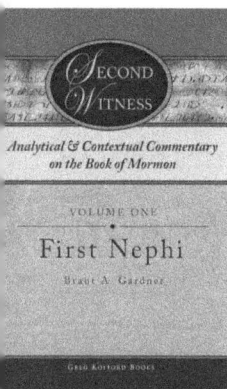

Second Witness:
Analytical and Contextual Commentatry on the Book of Mormon

Brant A. Gardner

Second Witness, a new six-volume series from Greg Kofford Books, takes a detailed, verse-by-verse look at the Book of Mormon. It marshals the best of modern scholarship and new insights into a consistent picture of the Book of Mormon as a historical document. Taking a faithful but scholarly approach to the text and reading it through the insights of linguistics, anthropology, and ethnohistory, the commentary approaches the text from a variety of perspectives: how it was created, how it relates to history and culture, and what religious insights it provides.

The commentary accepts the best modern scholarship, which focuses on a particular region of Mesoamerica as the most plausible location for the Book of Mormon's setting. For the first time, that location—its peoples, cultures, and historical trends—are used as the backdrop for reading the text. The historical background is not presented as proof, but rather as an explanatory context.

The commentary does not forget Mormon's purpose in writing. It discusses the doctrinal and theological aspects of the text and highlights the way in which Mormon created it to meet his goal of "convincing . . . the Jew and Gentile that Jesus is the Christ, the Eternal God."

Praise for the *Second Witness* series:

"Gardner not only provides a unique tool for understanding the Book of Mormon as an ancient document written by real, living prophets, but he sets a standard for Latter-day Saint thinking and writing about scripture, providing a model for all who follow. . . . No other reference source will prove as thorough and valuable for serious readers of the Book of Mormon."

-Neal A. Maxwell Institute, Brigham Young University

1st Nephi: 978-1-58958-041-1
2nd Nephi–Jacob: 978-1-58958-042-8
Enos–Mosiah: 978-1-58958-043-5

4. Alma: 978-1-58958-044-2
5. Helaman–3rd Nephi: 978-1-58958-045-9
6. 4th Nephi–Moroni: 978-1-58958-046-6

Complete set: 978-1-58958-047-3

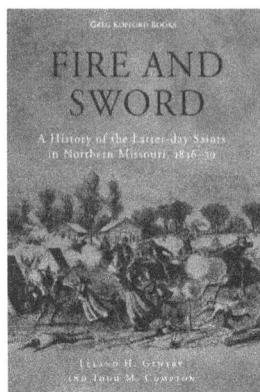

Fire and Sword:
A History of the Latter-day Saints in Northern Missouri, 1836-39

Leland Homer Gentry
and Todd M. Compton

Hardcover, ISBN: 978-1-58958-103-6

Many Mormon dreams flourished in Missouri. So did many Mormon nightmares.

The Missouri period—especially from the summer of 1838 when Joseph took over vigorous, personal direction of this new Zion until the spring of 1839 when he escaped after five months of imprisonment—represents a moment of intense crisis in Mormon history. Representing the greatest extremes of devotion and violence, commitment and intolerance, physical suffering and terror—mobbings, battles, massacres, and political "knockdowns"—it shadowed the Mormon psyche for a century.

Leland Gentry was the first to step beyond this disturbing period as a one-sided symbol of religious persecution and move toward understanding it with careful documentation and evenhanded analysis. In Fire and Sword, Todd Compton collaborates with Gentry to update this foundational work with four decades of new scholarship, more insightful critical theory, and the wealth of resources that have become electronically available in the last few years.

Compton gives full credit to Leland Gentry's extraordinary achievement, particularly in documenting the existence of Danites and in attempting to tell the Missourians' side of the story; but he also goes far beyond it, gracefully drawing into the dialogue signal interpretations written since Gentry and introducing the raw urgency of personal writings, eyewitness journalists and bemused politicians seesawing between human compassion and partisan harshness. In the lush Missouri landscape of the Mormon imagination where Adam and Eve had walked out of the garden and where Adam would return to preside over his posterity, the towering religious creativity of Joseph Smith and clash of religious stereotypes created a swift and traumatic frontier drama that changed the Church.

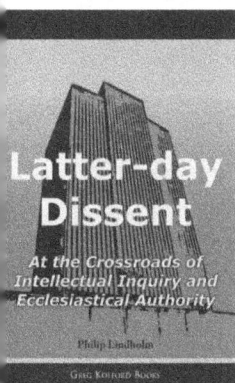

Latter-Day Dissent:
At the Crossroads of Intellectual
Inquiry and Ecclesiastical Authority

Philip Lindholm

Paperback, ISBN: 978-1-58958-128-9

This volume collects, for the first time in book form, stories from the "September Six," a group of intellectuals officially excommunicated or disfellowshipped from the LDS Church in September of 1993 on charges of "apostasy" or "conduct unbecoming" Church members. Their experiences are significant and yet are largely unknown outside of scholarly or more liberal Mormon circles, which is surprising given that their story was immediately propelled onto screens and cover pages across the Western world.

Interviews by Dr. Philip Lindholm (Ph.D. Theology, University of Oxford) include those of the "September Six," Lynne Kanavel Whitesides, Paul James Toscano, Maxine Hanks, Lavina Fielding Anderson, and D. Michael Quinn; as well as Janice Merrill Allred, Margaret Merrill Toscano, Thomas W. Murphy , and former employee of the LDS Church's Public Affairs Department, Donald B. Jessee.

Each interview illustrates the tension that often exists between the Church and its intellectual critics, and highlights the difficulty of accommodating congregational diversity while maintaining doctrinal unity—a difficulty hearkening back to the very heart of ancient Christianity.

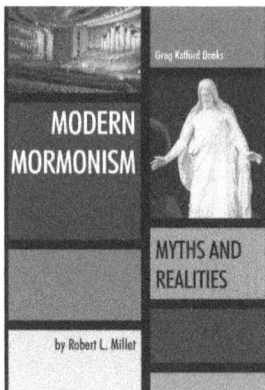

Modern Mormonism: Myths and Realities

Robert L. Millet

Paperback, ISBN: 978-1-58958-127-2

What answer may a Latter-day Saint make to accusations from those of other faiths that "Mormons aren't Christians," or "You think God is a man," and "You worship a different Jesus"? Not only are these charges disconcerting, but the hostility with which they are frequently hurled is equally likely to catch Latter-day Saints off guard.

Now Robert L. Millet, veteran of hundreds of such verbal battles, cogently, helpfully, and scripturally provides important clarifications for Latter-day Saints about eleven of the most frequent myths used to discredit the Church. Along the way, he models how to conduct such a Bible based discussion respectfully, weaving in enlightenment from LDS scriptures and quotation from religious figures in other faiths, ranging from the early church fathers to the archbishop of Canterbury.

Millet enlivens this book with personal experiences as a boy growing up in an area where Mormons were a minuscule and not particularly welcome minority, in one-on-one conversations with men of faith who believed differently, and with his own BYU students who also had lessons to learn about interfaith dialogue. He pleads for greater cooperation in dealing with the genuine moral and social evils afflicting the world, and concludes with his own ardent and reverent testimony of the Savior.

Hugh Nibley:
A Consecrated Life

Boyd Jay Petersen

Hardcover, ISBN: 978-1-58958-019-0

Winner of the Mormon History Association's Best Biography Award

As one of the LDS Church's most widely recognized scholars, Hugh Nibley is both an icon and an enigma. Through complete access to Nibley's correspondence, journals, notes, and papers, Petersen has painted a portrait that reveals the man behind the legend.

Starting with a foreword written by Zina Nibley Petersen and finishing with appendices that include some of the best of Nibley's personal correspondence, the biography reveals aspects of the tapestry of the life of one who has truly consecrated his life to the service of the Lord.

Praise for *A Consecrated Life*:

"Hugh Nibley is generally touted as one of Mormonism's greatest minds and perhaps its most prolific scholarly apologist. Just as hefty as some of Nibley's largest tomes, this authorized biography is delightfully accessible and full of the scholar's delicious wordplay and wit, not to mention some astonishing war stories and insights into Nibley's phenomenal acquisition of languages. Introduced by a personable foreword from the author's wife (who is Nibley's daughter), the book is written with enthusiasm, respect and insight. . . . On the whole, Petersen is a careful scholar who provides helpful historical context. . . . This project is far from hagiography. It fills an important gap in LDS history and will appeal to a wide Mormon audience."
> —Publishers Weekly

"Well written and thoroughly researched, Petersen's biography is a must-have for anyone struggling to reconcile faith and reason."
> —Greg Taggart, Association for Mormon Letters

The Gift and Power:
Translating the Book of Mormon

Brant A. Gardner

Hardcover, ISBN: 978-1-58958-131-9

From Brant A. Gardner, the author of the highly praised *Second Witne* commentaries on the Book of Mormon, comes *The Gift and Power: Translati the Book of Mormon*. In this first book-length treatment of the translatic process, Gardner closely examines the accounts surrounding Joseph Smitl translation of the Book of Mormon to answer a wide spectrum of question about the process, including: Did the Prophet use seerstones common to fo magicians of his time? How did he use them? And, what is the relationship the golden plates and the printed text?

Approaching the topic in three sections, part 1 examines the stories to about Joseph, folk magic, and the translation. Part 2 examines the availab evidence to determine how closely the English text replicates the original pla text. And part 3 seeks to explain how seer stones worked, why they no long work, and how Joseph Smith could have produced a translation with them.

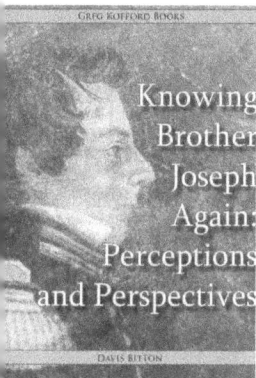

Knowing Brother Joseph Again: Perceptions and Perspectives

Davis Bitton

Hardcover, ISBN: 978-1-58958-123-4

In 1996, Davis Bitton, one of Mormon history's preeminent and much-loved scholars, published a collection of essays on Joseph Smith under the title, *Images of the Prophet Joseph Smith*. A decade later, when the book went out of print, Davis began work on an updated version that would also include some of his other work on the Mormon prophet. The project was only partially finished when his health failed. He died on April 13, 2007, at age seventy-seven. With the aid of additional historians, *Knowing Brother Joseph Again: Perceptions and Perspectives* brings to completion Davis's final work—a testament to his own admiration of the Prophet Joseph Smith.

From Davis Bitton's introducton:

This is not a conventional biography of Joseph Smith, but its intended purpose should not be hard to grasp. That purpose is to trace how Joseph Smith has appeared from different points of view. It is the image of Joseph Smith rather than the man himself that I seek to delineate.

Even when we have cut through the rumor and misinformation that surround all public figures and agree on many details, differences of interpretation remain. We live in an age of relativism. What is beautiful for one is not for another, what is good and moral for one is not for another, and what is true for one is not for another. I shudder at the thought that my presentation here will lead to such soft relativism.

Yet the fact remains that different people saw Joseph Smith in different ways. Even his followers emphasized different facets at different times. From their own perspectives, different people saw him differently or focused on different facet of his personality at different times. Inescapably, what they observed or found out about him was refracted through the lens of their own experience. Some of the different, flickering, not always compatible views are the subject of this book.

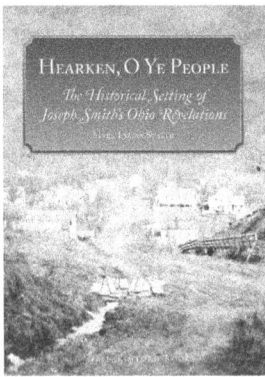

Hearken, O Ye People: The Historical Setting of Joseph Smith's Ohio Revelations

Mark Lyman Staker

Hardcover, ISBN: 978-1-58958-113-5

Awarded 2010 Best Book Award - John Whitmer Historical Association

More of Mormonism's canonized revelations originated in or near Kirtland than any other place. Yet many of the events connected with those revelations and their 1830s historical context have faded over time. Mark Staker reconstruct the cultural experiences by which Kirtland's Latter-day Saints made sense of th revelations Joseph Smith pronounced. This volume rebuilds that exciting decad using clues from numerous archives, privately held records, museum collection and even the soil where early members planted corn and homes. From this vas array of sources he shapes a detailed narrative of weather, religious background dialect differences, race relations, theological discussions, food preparation frontier violence, astronomical phenomena, and myriad daily customs c nineteenth-century life. The result is a "from the ground up" experience tha today's Latter-day Saints can all but walk into and touch.

Praise for *Hearken O Ye People*:

"I am not aware of a more deeply researched and richly contextualized stud of any period of Mormon church history than Mark Staker's study of Mormon in Ohio. We learn about everything from the details of Alexander Campbell views on priesthood authority to the road conditions and weather on the fou Lamanite missionaries' journey from New York to Ohio. All the Ohio revelation and even the First Vision are made to pulse with new meaning. This book sets new standard of in-depth research in Latter-day Saint history."

-Richard Bushman, author of *Joseph Smith: Rough Stone Rolling*

"To be well-informed, any student of Latter-day Saint history and doctrine mu now be acquainted with the remarkable research of Mark Staker on the importan history of the church in the Kirtland, Ohio, area."

-Neal A. Maxwell Institute, Brigham Young University

www.ingramcontent.com/pod-product-compliance
Lightning Source LLC
Chambersburg PA
CBHW072353090426
42741CB00012B/3023